AMERICAN BOOK ENGLISH

American Book Company

H. Thompson Fillmer   Ann Lefcourt   Nell C. Thompson

For Acknowledgments and Credits, see page 326.

American Book Company

New York   Cincinnati   Atlanta   Dallas   San Francisco

ISBN 0-278-48251-1

3   5   7   9   11   13   14   12   10   8   6   4   2

CONTENTS

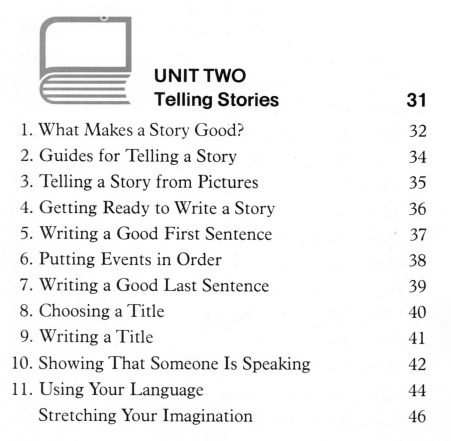

UNIT TWO
Telling Stories   31

UNIT THREE
Learning About Nouns and Pronouns   **55**

UNIT FOUR
Friendly Letters   **85**

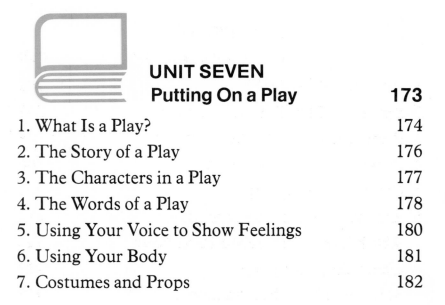

**UNIT SEVEN
Putting On a Play**   **173**

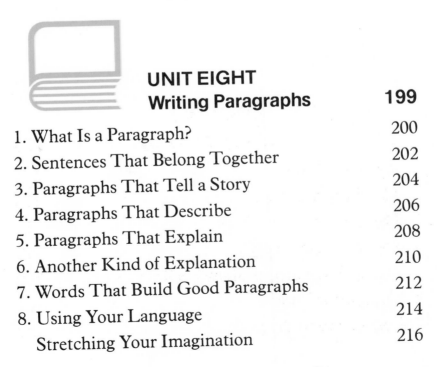

UNIT EIGHT
Writing Paragraphs **199**

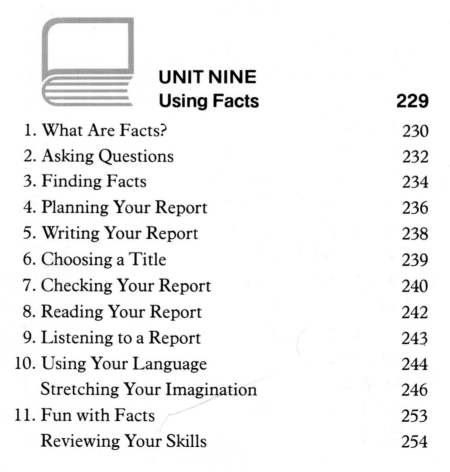

UNIT NINE
Using Facts — 229

Building Sentences

In this unit, you will look at letters, words, and sentences. Then you will learn about the two important parts of the sentence. You will make sentences grow by adding words, and you will practice writing two different kinds of sentences.

1 Telling Things

There are many different ways that you can tell someone something. Look at the picture on pages 2–3. What does it make you think of? Suppose you want to tell someone that you are hungry. Think of the different ways you can do that. The following girls and boys can help you.

1. Jeannette had a toothache and couldn't speak. But she was hungry. So she rubbed her stomach and made funny noises.

2. Carol was pretending not to speak to her father. But she was hungry. So she drew a picture of a big plate of spaghetti and showed it to him.

3. Walter was at camp, and he was always hungry. So he wrote a letter home. In the letter he wrote: "Send some food, please. I'm hungry."

4. Vinnie was hungry. So he went to his mother and said, "Mom, I'm hungry."

How did Jeannette and Carol show that they were hungry? Did either girl use words? How did Walter and Vinnie show that they were hungry? Did they use words? What kind of words did Walter use? What kind of words did Vinnie use?

If you want to tell someone something, you can do any one of the following things:

1. Move your body and make noises.
2. Draw a picture.
3. Write words.
4. Speak words.

Exercise A

Think of something you want to tell the class. Tell it without using words.

Exercise B

Pretend that you are in the picture on pages 2-3. Show how you would order something to eat.

Exercise C

Do Exercises A and B again. This time use words.

2 Sign Language

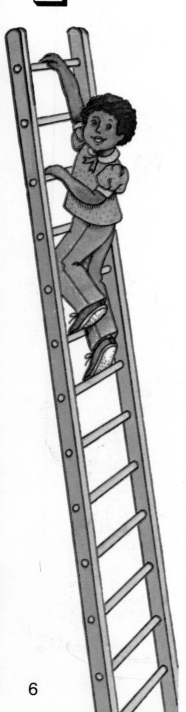

Pictures can show things and tell stories. But there are some things and ideas that pictures cannot show. Is the girl in this picture going up or down the ladder? You would have to draw more than one picture to show which way she is going. Or you could use signs. Here are two different kinds of signs:

1. Signs that show things look like the things they name.

cat   dog   house   tree   ladder   girl

boy   rain   sun   moon   water   fish

2. Signs that show ideas show them clearly.

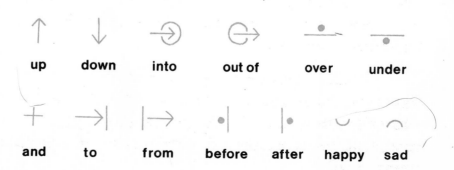

up   down   into   out of   over   under

and   to   from   before   after   happy   sad

Look at this story in sign language:

sun over house   **girl and boy out of house**

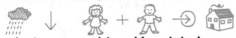

rain down   **girl and boy into house**

Use the words and the signs to tell what is happening.

Exercise A

Here is another story in sign language. Study the signs on page 6. Then tell what happens in this story. Each sentence is numbered.

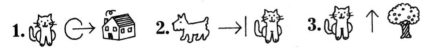

Exercise B

Make up your own story in sign language. Use the signs on page 6. You may also make up some of your own signs. Then show your story to the class and have them read it.

There is another kind of sign language. It is not a language you write or draw. It is the kind of language being used by the people shown at the right. What is each person shown at the right telling you to do?

7

3 Letters in Order

Look at this sentence from the story in sign language on page 7:

If you were telling the story in words, you would not say, "Cat up tree." What would you say? Suppose you said, "The cat ran up the tree." The sentence in sign language has only three signs. How many words are in the spoken sentence?

You can use a few signs to tell a story in sign language. But you need more words to tell a story when you speak. Letters help you to make the words that you cannot show with signs. You write words with letters.

Which of these groups of letters are words? Which are not words? Why are some groups of letters not words?

hto   glad   rdib   hello   oogd

Letters must be in a certain order to make a word.

Exercise A

Change the order of the letters in each group below to make a word. Then read the words you made. Read from left to right.

eht   gdo   anr   fater   het   tca
hte   atc   rna   pu   teh   etre

Exercise B

Here are some things you can do to show how much you know about letters and words.

1. Write as many words as you can, using only the letters in the following word:

   A L P H A B E T

2. Write a word that sounds like each of the following letters:

   B C J R T U Y

3. Write as many letters as you can in each box to make different words.

   a. ba☐   **c.** ☐ace

   b. ca☐e   **d.** ☐old

4. Change the order of the letters in each of the words below to make a new word. Use the picture clues at the right.

   a. act   **c.** stop   **e.** team

   b. gab   **d.** but   **f.** gum

5. Write the same letter in each pair of boxes below to make a word. The word clues will help you.

   a. ☐u☐   A small dog

   b. ☐a☐   Another word for *father*

   c. ☐i☐   An apron for a baby

   d. ☐ee☐   Noise made by a baby chick

   e. ☐oo☐   The middle of the day

9

4 Words in Order

What do you have to do with these letters to make a word? Do it.

o   r   w   d

What do you have to do with these words to make a sentence? Do it.

sleep   in   bears   caves

Words must be in a certain order to make a sentence.

Exercise A

Put each group of words below in the right order to make a sentence.

1. sun   hot   the   was
2. the   was   water   cold
3. found   nuts   some   we
4. by   grew   stream   some   a   flowers
5. loudly   bees   the   buzzed
6. deer   us   a   at   looked

Sometimes, you can make two different sentences with the same words. Look at these two sentences:

1. The snake hissed at the goose.
2. The goose hissed at the snake.

How are these two sentences the same? How are they different? Do they mean the same thing?

When you change the order of the words in a sentence, you sometimes change the meaning of the sentence.

Exercise B

Change the order of the words in each sentence below to change the meaning.

1. Molly laughed at the clown.
2. Jack went to see Sonia.
3. Cats like to chase dogs.
4. The gray house had a red roof.

Look at these two sentences.

1. We slowly walked home.
2. We walked home slowly.

How are these two sentences the same? How are they different? Do they mean the same thing?

Sometimes, changing the order of the words does not change the meaning of the sentence.

Exercise C

Change the order of the words in each sentence below without changing the meaning.

1. One of my friends is Angela.
2. The fire quickly warmed us.
3. Suddenly the storm broke.
4. The last song was the best one.

5 The Parts of a Sentence

Look at this sentence:

Dogs bark.

The first word in the sentence tells what the sentence is about. The word *Dogs* is the subject of the sentence.

The subject of a sentence tells what the sentence is about.

Look at the sentence about the dogs again. The second word in the sentence tells something about the subject. The word *bark* is the predicate of the sentence.

The predicate of a sentence tells something about the subject.

CAREER CLUES

I use hand signs and my whistle to make cars stop and go. People depend on me to keep them safe. I am a _____.

Exercise A

Write the sentences below. Draw a slash mark (/) between the subject and the predicate of each sentence.

1. Geese honk.
2. Leaves fall.
3. Roberto sang.
4. Cork floats.
5. Rocks sink.
6. Inez won.

The subject of a sentence can be one word or more than one word. Look at these sentences.

1. Bees / buzz.
2. The bee / buzzed.

The words on the left of each slash mark make up the subject of the sentence.

The predicate of a sentence can also be one word or more than one word. Look at these sentences:

1. The birds / sang.
2. The birds / sang sweetly.

The words on the right of each slash mark make up the predicate of the sentence.

Exercise B

Write these sentences. Draw a slash mark between the subject and the predicate of each sentence.

1. My aunt lives in Scranton.
2. Her family owns a house under a bridge.
3. Trucks roar across the bridge.
4. The wheels make a lot of noise.
5. A big green truck rumbled by.
6. The windows shook.
7. The baby cried.
8. My uncle picked her up.

13

6 The Key Word in the Subject

Look at this sentence:

Many old trees / grow in the park.

What is the subject of the sentence? Every subject has a key word. Why is *trees* the key word in the subject "Many old trees"?

The key word in the subject names the person, animal, place, thing, or idea that the sentence is about.

Exercise

In each sentence below, the key word is missing from the subject. Talk about interesting words that can be used for each box.

1. The last ☐ leaves at eight o'clock.
2. My ☐ read two books last week.
3. A little gray ☐ sat on the fence.
4. The ☐ waited for ten minutes.
5. The ☐ knew the answer.
6. The two ☐ looked in the room.
7. My ☐ wrote a funny story.
8. The ☐ hopped through the gate.
9. The ☐ ran for the bus.
10. A big ☐ swam in the tank.

The Key Word in the Predicate 7

Read the sentence about the trees again:

Many old trees / grow in the park.

What is the predicate of the sentence? Every predicate has a key word. Why is *grow* the key word in the predicate "grow in the park"?

The key word in the predicate tells what the subject does or is.

Exercise

In each sentence below, the key word is missing from the predicate. Talk about interesting words that can be used for each box.

1. A strong wind ☐ the tree down.
2. Frightened animals ☐ through the woods.
3. A woman ☐ along the sidewalk.
4. A car ☐ around the corner.
5. A police officer ☐ the cat.
6. The clown ☐ at the children.
7. A rabbit ☐ out of the bushes.
8. The children ☐ in the field.
9. The girls ☐ the car.
10. The team ☐ the game.

Facts About Language

About 200 alphabets have been used by different people in the past. Today more than 50 different alphabets are in use.

15

8 Making Sentences Grow

Look at these two sentences:

1. Ducks quacked.
2. The big wet ducks quacked.

What is the subject of each sentence? What is one way to make sentences grow?

You can make a sentence grow by adding words to the subject.

Exercise A

Make each sentence grow by adding words to the subject.

1. Trucks roared.　**2.** Cars stopped.　**3.** People ran.

Look at these two sentences:

1. The ducks quacked.
2. The ducks quacked loudly.

What is the predicate of each sentence? What is another way to make sentences grow?

You can make a sentence grow by adding words to the predicate.

Exercise B

Make each sentence in Exercise A grow by adding words to the predicate.

Writing Statements 9

What do sentences do? Different kinds of sentences do different things. Some sentences tell you something. They are called *statements*. Other sentences ask you something. They are called *questions*.

Look at this sentence:

Spring is almost here.

Is this sentence a statement or a question? With what kind of letter does the statement begin? With what mark does it end?

A statement is a sentence that tells something. A statement begins with a capital letter and ends with a period.

Exercise A

Write these statements correctly:

1. the day was muggy
2. richard made some iced tea
3. carlotta called him on the phone
4. he left the ice cubes on the sink
5. they melted

Exercise B

Look at the pictures on this page. Make up a statement about each picture. In your statement tell what the boy or girl is doing.

10 Writing Questions

Look at the sentence below. Does it tell you something or ask you something?

Can you dance?

Is this sentence a statement or a question? With what kind of letter does the question begin? With what mark does it end?

A question is a sentence that asks something. A question begins with a capital letter and ends with a question mark.

Exercise A

Write these questions correctly:

1. who will dance with me
2. can you do this step
3. where are the records
4. have you heard the latest hit
5. what do you think of it

Sometimes a question begins with a question word. *Who, What, When, Where, How,* and *Why* are question words.

Exercise B

Look at the pictures on page 17. Make up a question about each picture.

MORE PRACTICE

A. On your paper, write the following as statements:

1. pedro is my friend
2. he visits me every summer
3. we do many exciting things
4. i have a surprise for him
5. our dog had puppies

B. Write the following as questions:

1. where is the book fair
2. who is having it
3. what time does it start
4. are you going
5. may I buy a book

C. Some of the sentences below are statements, and some are questions. Write them correctly on your paper.

1. how far away is the bus station
2. we are driving there today
3. my mom is coming home
4. can you come with us
5. dad won't mind

D. Write each of the following sentences as a statement. Then write each one as a question. Read your sentences aloud.

1. these are fresh peas
2. your father will pick you up
3. she will win the contest
4. we are having steak tonight
5. rita can speak two languages

19

You already know that the first word in a sentence begins with a capital letter. Look at the sentences below. What other words begin with capital letters? Why?

1. My snake Goops likes Bonnie and me.
2. Why do I like Goops?

Which word in sentence 1 names a pet? Which word names a person? Which word in sentence 2 is always written with a capital letter?

The name of a pet or a person always begins with a capital letter. The word _I_ is always a capital letter.

Exercise

Write each sentence. Use capital letters where they are needed. Use a period or question mark at the end.

1. my sister annette has a pet mouse
2. the mouse's name is marty
3. one day, david came to visit us
4. he and i are good friends
5. but david doesn't like marty
6. does gloria have many pets
7. she has a snake called sam
8. why does gloria carry sam around her neck

Each unit in your book has an editing exercise. *Editing* is another way of saying "checking for mistakes." Before you hand in a paper, remember to do the following:

1. Look for mistakes you know you make over and over again. The editing exercise will remind you of certain things to look for.

2. Make a clean copy of what you write before you hand it in.

Edit each sentence below by asking yourself these questions: (a) Does the sentence begin with a capital letter? (b) Does it end with the correct mark? (c) Are capital letters used where they are needed?

1. books are fun to read
2. what kind of books do you read
3. may i use the dictionary
4. marshall works in the library
5. his sister eleanor is an editor
6. i read the newspaper every day
7. when do you study
8. sparky chewed up my notebook
9. did you read ramon's poem
10. who wrote that ghost story

EDITING EXERCISE

12 Working with Words

Using Words That Give a Clear Picture

You have just explored different kinds of sentences. You learned that the subject and the predicate can be one word or more than one word. Read these sentences:

1. Person / went.
2. The person / went into the building.

What picture did you see when you read sentence 2? What word for *person* would make the picture clearer? What word for *went* would make the picture clearer? What word for *building* would make the picture clearer? The exercises on this page and on page 23 will help you write sentences that give clear pictures.

Exercise A

Read sentence 2 again. Think about different words for *person*. Make a list of words like *girl, boy, man,* and *woman* that give a clearer picture of who went into the building. Choose a word from the list. Save your word for Exercise D.

Exercise B

Read sentence 2 again. Think about different words for *building*. Add to the list of different kinds of buildings given below. Choose a word from the list. Save your word for Exercise D.

house   school   factory   castle

Exercise C

Read sentence 2 again. Think about different words for *went*. Add to the list given below. Choose a word from the list. Save your word for Exercise D.

stepped   tiptoed   limped   skipped
ran   raced   crawled strolled

Exercice D

Use the words you chose from the lists in Exercises A, B, and C to write a sentence that gives a clear picture.

Exercice E

Look at the picture on this page. Write a sentence that gives a clear picture of what is happening.

23

Look at these pictures:

What do you use a fork for? What do you use a knife for? What do you use a spoon for? Forks, knives, and spoons are tools that you use to eat.

Now look at these pictures:

Which eating tool would you use with each of the foods shown? Tell why. Then tell why the other eating tools would not work as well.

Some tools do what you want better than others.

 Exercise A

Tell what each of the following tools does best. Then think of some things these tools would *not* do well.

hammer   needle   scissors
pencil   eraser   ruler

Words are tools, too. Some words work better than others. Which word—*saw* or *seen*—would you use in this sentence?

I ☐ a shooting star.

Some people who speak English sometimes say, "I seen a shooting star." However, most people most of the time say, "I saw a shooting star." If you say, "I seen a shooting star," many people might think that you don't know which words to use.

Choosing the Right Word

Some words do what you want better than others.

There are many words in English that present you with a choice. Other lessons in this book will help you with some of these choices. But, for now, do the following exercise.

Exercise B

Look at the pictures on this page. Your teacher will help you talk about them.

25

Reviewing Your Skills

The page numerals after each heading show you where to look if you need help with this review.

Putting Letters in Order (8–9)

Change the order of the letters in each group below to make the name of an animal.

1. ered   3. akesn   5. brabit
2. puypp   4. ynop   6. tac

Putting Words in Order (10–11)

Change the order of the words in each group below to make a sentence.

1. cousin my delivers papers
2. works Mom in hospital a
3. friend helped her a
4. stopped cars the at corner the
5. club nine belong to people the

Dividing Sentences Into Two Parts (12–13)

Write each sentence below. Draw a slash mark between the subject and the predicate.

1. Three dogs raced around the block.
2. My sister made a racing car.
3. The boys played a new game.
4. The wheel bumped into the curb.
5. A cab stood in the rain.
6. Many boats sailed on the river.
7. My cousin lives in West Virginia.
8. The stars twinkle in the sky.

Finding Key Words (14–15)

Write each sentence. Draw one line under the key word in the subject. Draw two lines under the key word in the predicate.

1. A woman climbed up the ladder.
2. The player dropped the ball.
3. Two horses pulled the wagon.
4. An old woman fed the birds.
5. Black smoke came out of the chimney.

Writing Statements and Questions (17–18)

A. Write each group of words below as a statement.

1. your dog is a stray
2. my brother is here
3. it is raining hard
4. grandma will help us
5. dad is leaving early

B. Write each group of words in Part A as a question.

Using Capital Letters (20)

Write each sentence. Use capital letters where they are needed. Use a period or question mark at the end.

1. my brother joe has a friend
2. the friend's name is cora
3. both cora and i like fish
4. her fish snapper had babies
5. may i feed snapper

Testing Your Skills

Putting Letters in Order

Change the order of the letters in each word below to make a new word.

1. palm   **3.** tale   **5.** owl

2. vase   **4.** lap   **6.** sue

Putting Words in Order

Change the order of the words in each group below to make a sentence.

1. used language picture people

2. told the stories pictures

3. for pictures stood words

4. picture words people differently

5. see pictures people differently

6. picture every understand may we not

7. picture one could several things mean

8. meaning one seem to you may right

Dividing Sentences Into Two Parts

Write each sentence below. Draw a slash mark between the subject and the predicate.

1. Our school won the contest.

2. The pitcher threw a fast ball.

3. A feather floated in the breeze.

4. My mother painted the house.

5. His friend lives near the park.

6. The baby played with the blocks.

7. My aunt delivers papers on Saturday.

8. The carpenter fixed the door.

Finding Key Words

Write each sentence. Draw one line under the key word in the subject. Draw two lines under the key word in the predicate.

1. The children laughed at the clowns.
2. A blue truck roared into the tunnel.
3. A big crowd gathered on the corner.
4. A strong wind rattled the windows.
5. A small stream flows past our house.

Writing Statements and Questions

A. Write each group of words below as a statement.

1. it will snow all day
2. we are having a test
3. your brother is a catcher
4. that is my jacket
5. the show will be over soon

B. Write each group of words in Part A as a question.

Using Capital Letters

Write each sentence. Use capital letters where they are needed. Use a period or question mark at the end.

1. my cousin carlos and i are good friends
2. he and i have a dog named curly
3. where do we walk curly
4. carlos and i run in the park with curly
5. a friend sue cheng runs with us

Telling Stories

COMPOSITION   Writing a Good
                    Beginning
                   Putting Events in Order
                   Writing a Good Ending
                   Choosing a Title

SPEAKING   Telling a Story in Class

MECHANICS   Using Quotation Marks
                   Writing a Title

USAGE   Naming Yourself Last

In this unit, you will learn how to tell and write a story. You will discover how to show that a character in your story is speaking. After reading a story by a famous storyteller, you will make some unusual characters speak.

1 What Makes a Story Good?

The statue in the picture on pages 30–31 is of a famous storyteller. The stories that Hans Christian Andersen wrote can be read in almost every language. In the lessons that follow, you will learn some of the things Hans Christian Andersen knew about telling stories.

There are many different kinds of stories. Some stories, like those told by Hans Christian Andersen, are about make-believe people and things. Others are about real people and things. Some stories are sad. Some are funny. Some stories tell about great adventures. Others tell about everyday happenings.

All good stories have three things in common. What are they? Here are some clues to help you:

1. Lou couldn't think of a first sentence for his story, so he began in the middle.
2. Abigail mixed up the order of things in her story.
3. Frank's story was good until he got toward the end. Then he just stopped.

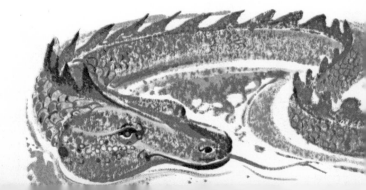

Exercise

Talk about the answers to these questions:

1. Why is the first sentence of a story important?
2. Why is it important to keep the things that happen in a story in the right order?
3. Why is the last sentence of a story important?

Remember these guides when you write a story:

1. Think of a good first sentence that will make the reader want to read the whole story.

2. Put the things that happen in the story in the right order so that the story is easier to understand.

3. Think of a good last sentence that will help the reader remember the story.

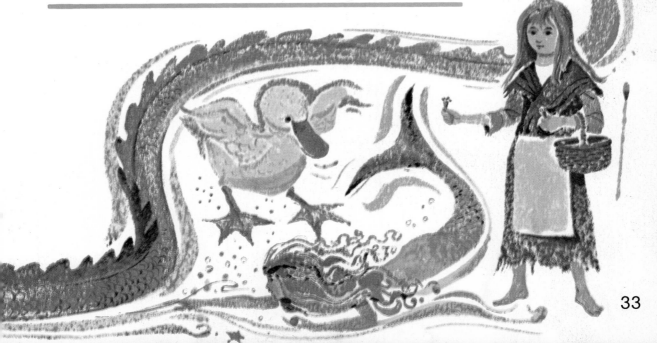

2 Guides for Telling a Story

When you tell a story, you want your listeners to understand and enjoy the story. What is the best way to tell a story? Here are some clues to help you.

1. Andy spoke so fast, no one could understand him. Tara spoke so softly, no one could hear her.
2. Meg kept looking out the window. No one could get interested in her story.
3. Alonzo's story was fine, but he kept moving around. No one paid attention to his story.

 Exercise

Talk about the answers to these questions:

1. How should you speak when you tell a story?
2. Where should you look when you tell a story?
3. How should you stand when you tell a story?

Remember these guides when you tell a story.

1. Speak clearly and slowly so that your listeners can hear and understand you.

2. Look at your listeners when you tell your story.

3. Don't move around too much when you tell your story.

Telling a Story from Pictures 3

A cartoon strip is a group of pictures that tell a story. Look at the cartoon strip below. Think about what is happening. Take turns telling the story.

1.

2.

3.

4.

© 1960 by United Feature Syndicate, Inc.

Exercise

Find a cartoon strip that tells a story with just a few words. Think about the story it tells. Then tell your story to the class. Use the guides on pages 33 and 34.

You can also tell a story from just one picture. Look at the picture on pages 30–31. Think about a story you can tell from the picture. You may have to make up some parts of the story not shown in the picture. Talk about story ideas in class.

Getting Ready to Write a Story

Before you write a story, think about what you are going to write. What are some of the things you should know about your story before you write it? Here are some questions that will help you.

1. *Who* is in the story?
2. *Where* does the story take place?
3. *When* does the story happen?
4. *What* happens in the story?

When you talk about the people in a story, you are talking about the characters.

When you talk about what happens in a story, you are talking about the events.

 Exercise A

Think about a story you know. Then use the four questions above to talk about the story in class.

Now you are ready to think about writing your own story. Exercise B will help you get started.

Exercise B

Think about something that really happened to you. Then ask yourself the four questions above. Write your answers on a piece of paper. Keep your answers for the lessons that follow.

36

Writing a Good First Sentence 5

On page 33, what is the first guide for telling a story? Here are two different first sentences for the same story. Talk about which sentence makes you want to read the whole story and why.

1. This is a story about a dog.
2. Last week, Polly had an adventure with her dog Conrad.

The first sentence is not very interesting. It doesn't tell you much. The second sentence is much more interesting. It tells you who some of the characters in the story are. It tells you when the story happened. It tells you that the story is an adventure. But it doesn't tell you what that adventure is. A good first sentence tells you just enough so that you want to read on.

Facts About Language

The language of signs is older than the language of words.

Exercise A

Read the sentences below. Which sentence is the better first sentence for the same story. Why?

1. This girl I know is really funny.
2. Monica's jokes in class almost got her in trouble last Tuesday.

Exercise B

Look at what you wrote for Exercise B on page 36. Use your answers to help you write a good first sentence for your story.

37

6 Putting Events in Order

FUTURE

first

next

then

last

today

yesterday

morning

afternoon

PAST

On page 33, what is the second guide for telling a story? Read the story below. Are the events in order?

On my way home, I found my watch on the sidewalk near the bus stop. I lost my watch this morning on my way to school. When I looked at my wrist, the watch was gone. I remember Jerry asking me what time it was. I can't believe how lucky I was.

Which sentence tells when the watch was lost? Which sentence tells what made the owner discover that the watch was missing? When was the watch found? Does the story begin at the beginning?

Exercise A

Rewrite the story about the lost watch. Put the events in the right order.

Certain words can help you show the order of events in a story. Some of these words are listed at the left. What do these words show? Words that show time can help you put the events of a story in the right order.

Exercise B

Look at what you wrote for Exercise B on page 36. Use time words to put the events of your story in order.

Writing a Good Last Sentence 7

On page 33, what is the third guide for telling a story? There are different kinds of good last sentences. Look at the two sentences below. Sentence 1 is the first sentence of a story. Sentence 2 is the last sentence of the same story.

1. I've always wondered why Tonio smiles all the time.
2. Now I know why Tonio smiles all the time.

A good last sentence often repeats the idea of the first sentence.

Now read the story below.

George surprised Maryann with the news. He told her that he had a book that contained every word of a story she had written. She didn't believe him and asked to see the book. He opened his desk and pulled out a dictionary.

A good last sentence is often a joke or a surprise.

 Exercise

Write your story. Follow these steps:

1. Use the first sentence you wrote for Exercise B on page 37.
2. Use the order of events you wrote for Exercise B on page 38.
3. Write a good last sentence.

39

Everything has a name. Even stories have names. The name of a story is its title.

The title of a story is the first thing a reader sees. A good title is like a good first sentence. If the title is interesting, the reader will want to read the story. A title should also tell just enough about the story so that the reader wants to know more.

Exercise A

Which of the titles below are good titles? Tell why.

1. A Prize for the Pony
2. A Funny Story
3. Some of My Toys
4. The Midnight Race

Exercise B

Read the following story and make up a title for it. Then talk about your titles in class.

One night I heard a strange noise in the living room. Someone was playing the piano. It was late and everyone in the family was in bed. Who could it be? I got up and crept downstairs. The living room was dark. When I turned on the light, my cat jumped off the piano and ran under a chair. Now I call her my musical cat.

Look at the titles in Exercise A on page 40. Which words in each title begin with capital letters? What kinds of words do not begin with capital letters? The first word, the last word, and all important words in a title begin with capital letters.

Now look at these titles:

1. A Tired Bicycle   2. Who Owns the Sun?

A title never ends with a period. A title that asks a question ends with a question mark.

Remember these guidelines for writing titles:

1. Begin the first word, the last word, and each important word with a capital letter.

2. Use a question mark at the end of a title that asks a question.

Exercise A

Write these titles correctly.

1. the sounds of spring
2. a road to freedom
3. adventure on the roof
4. was it a ghost

Exercise B

Make up titles for the stories you have written in class. Write them correctly.

10 Showing That Someone Is Speaking

Look at this sentence from a story:

Lisa said, "My arms are tired."

Who is speaking in this sentence? What are the exact words Lisa said? What marks are used to show her exact words? Quotation marks are used in a story to show the exact words of a speaker.

The following steps will help you show that the characters in your story are speaking:

1. Write the exact words of the speaker. Use capital letters and end marks where they are needed.

   My arms are tired.

2. Put quotation marks around the exact words of the speaker and the end mark.

   "My arms are tired."

3. Write the name of the speaker and the word *said* before the exact words.

   Lisa said "My arms are tired."

4. Put a comma between the word *said* and the exact words of the speaker.

   Lisa said, "My arms are tired."

Talk about other words you can use in place of *said.* Here are some ideas:

asked   shouted   answered   cried

Write each sentence below as the exact words of a speaker. Make up a name for each speaker and write the sentences correctly.

1. I don't want to play this game.
2. What do you want to do?
3. Let's go to a movie.
4. Do you have any money?
5. I'm broke.

Look at these sentences from a story. Notice where each sentence begins.

> Chris said, "I'm going to the library to get a book on farming."
> Marta asked, "Why do you want a book on farming?"
> Chris answered, "I want to start a garden."

Each time there is a new speaker in a story, the sentence begins on a new line. The first word on the new line is indented.

Exercise B

Write a story in which two characters speak. Use capital letters, commas, quotation marks, and end marks where they are needed. Remember to begin a new line and indent it when the speaker changes.

11 Using Your Language

Read these sentences from a story:

1. Jane and I ran through the woods.
2. The bear chased Jane and me.

When you write about yourself and someone else, remember to name yourself last.

Exercise A

Read each sentence. Use someone's name and the word *I* for the box. Use a different name for each sentence.

1. ☑ planned a picnic.
2. ☐ live on the same block.
3. ☐ went to the beach.
4. ☐ flew to San Juan.
5. ☐ watched the game on TV.

Exercise B

Read each sentence. Use someone's name and the word *me* for the box. Use a different name for each sentence.

1. Mom helped ☐.
2. Aunt Lisa gave the books to ☐.
3. Dad made dinner for ☐.
4. The teacher showed ☐ the new fish tank.
5. The dog followed ☐ to school.

Exercise C

Use the name of a friend and the word *I* in this sentence: ☐ *went to the zoo.* Add more sentences to tell a story about what happened to you and your friend.

Naming Yourself Last

The story below needs editing. One sentence should be left out. Capital letters and end marks are missing. In one place the speaker changes, but the writer forgot to begin a new line and indent it. Write the story so that it is interesting and correct.

This is my story. it was the first day of summer vacation and it was raining. I and dolores sat by the window and watched the rain.
    i sighed and said what should we do
    dolores said i have an idea let's have a raindrop race i asked what's a raindrop race
    dolores answered we each watch a raindrop on the window and see which drop gets to the bottom first
    so i and dolores enjoyed the first day of summer vacation after all

EDITING EXERCISE

Earlier in this unit, you met the famous storyteller who wrote the tale you are about to read. As you will see, a good storyteller *writes* with imagination. Get ready to stretch your imagination as you *read* about an unusual contest. In the lesson that follows, you will be asked to stretch your imagination in a different way.

The Jumping Contest

A flea, a grasshopper, and a jumping jack decided to hold a contest. They wanted to see who could jump the highest. They invited the whole world to watch them.

"I will give a bag of gold to the one who jumps the highest," said the king.

The flea introduced himself first. He had very fine manners. But then he was used to being with people. Then came the grasshopper. He was plump and dressed in a fine green uniform. He said that his family came from Egypt. "I sing so well," he boasted, "that all the crickets have left the country."

The jumping jack came last. He was made from the wishbone of a chicken, two rubber bands, some glue, and a stick. He had nothing to say.

STRETCHING

The contest began. The flea jumped so high that no one could see him. The king said that he hadn't jumped at all.

The grasshopper jumped half as high as the flea. He landed right in the king's face, and that made the king very angry indeed.

Now it was the jumping jack's turn. He gave a little jump but high enough to land in the lap of the king's favorite child. The little princess laughed and began to play with the jumping jack.

"The jumping jack is the winner," said the king. "The bag of gold is his."

The flea was so angry that, like the crickets, he left the country. The grasshopper sat down in a ditch and sang his own sad song. It is from him that we have the story of the flea, the grasshopper, and the jumping jack.

YOUR IMAGINATION

12 Writing with Imagination

Here is your chance to find out what can happen when you stretch your imagination. Instead of reading about insects and objects that talk, you will write about them.

Exercise A

Talk about the talking insects and animals you met in "The Jumping Contest." Do you have a dog, cat, fish, or other pet? If your pet could talk, what would it say?

Exercise B

Think of an idea for a story like "The Jumping Contest." In your story, do the following things:

1. Make use of two or more talking animals or objects.
2. Have the animals and objects talk to humans.
3. Think of something interesting that happens to your characters.

Exercise C

Now write your story. Remember to give it a title. When you finish your story, edit it and make corrections. Did you use quotation marks and other marks correctly?

Reviewing Your Skills

The page numerals after each heading show you where to look if you need help with this review.

Choosing a Good First Sentence (37)

Write the sentence that would make a good first sentence for a story.

1. a. The street was dark and wet.
   b. This is a story about my block.

2. a. My dog is cute.
   b. Wags can do three tricks.

Putting Events in Order (38)

Put the events below in order.

1. Children hear kitten
2. Children in woods
3. Children carry kitten home
4. Children find kitten in bushes
5. Owner thanks children

Choosing a Good Last Sentence (39)

Write the sentence that would make a good last sentence for a story.

1. a. That is how I learned to swim.
   b. I can do the dog paddle and everything.

2. a. Sisters are nice.
   b. That is why my sister is my best friend.

Writing Titles (41)

Write each title. Use capital letters where they are needed.

1. my new bike
2. up on the roof
3. baking a cake
4. a party for snoopy
5. on the fire truck
6. a walk in the rain

Showing That Someone Is Speaking (42–43)

Write the sentences below. Use commas, capital letters, and quotation marks to show that someone is speaking.

1. alice shouted come back, tiger
2. tom asked is that your cat in the mailbox
3. alice said you are a bad cat
4. she scolded you must not run away

Using Your Language (44–45)

Write each sentence. In sentences 1 to 3, use someone's name and the word *I* for the box. In sentences 4 to 6, use someone's name and the word *me*.

1. ☐ hurried home.
2. ☐ rode our bikes.
3. ☐ raked the leaves.
4. The teacher smiled at ☐.
5. Dad helped ☐.
6. She gave the book to ☐.

Testing Your Skills

Writing Titles

Write each title. Use capital letters where they are needed.

1. all dressed up
2. a trip to the city
3. our new car
4. watching the stars
5. a funny pet
6. a picnic in the park

Showing That Someone Is Speaking

Write the sentences below. Use commas, capital letters, and quotation marks to show that someone is speaking.

1. mark asked why did the chicken cross the road
2. betty answered he wanted to get to the other side
3. mark asked did we both read the same joke book
4. betty answered i think so

Putting Events in Order

Write the events below in order.

1. Child running across street
2. Parents thanking girl
3. Girl rescuing child
4. Girl stopping traffic

Writing a Story

Write the story that the pictures below tell. Before you start to write, think about the following:

1. A good first sentence **3.** A good last sentence

2. Four events in the story **4.** A good title

Using Your Language

Write each sentence. In sentences 1 to 3, use someone's name and the word *me* for the box. In sentences 4 to 6, use someone's name and the word *I*.

1. They saw ☐.

2. A dog followed ☐.

3. Bob borrowed a book from ☐.

4. ☐ went to the fair.

5. ☐ played ball.

6. ☐ minded the baby.

Skills Checkup

Dividing Sentences Into Two Parts (12–13)

Write each sentence below. Draw a slash mark between the subject and the predicate.

1. The boys made a cake.
2. My aunt writes stories.
3. The coach blew her whistle.
4. Our rabbit ran away.

Finding Key Words (14–15)

Write each sentence. Draw one line under the key word in the subject. Draw two lines under the key word in the predicate.

1. The days flew by.
2. My cousin visits us every year.
3. Their friends joined a club.
4. The fire burned all night.

Writing Statements and Questions (17–18)

Write each group of words below as a statement or a question. Use capital letters where they are needed.

1. have you seen my dog
2. jan and i saw him on the next block
3. where is jan
4. we looked everywhere for spot

53

Learning About Nouns and Pronouns

GRAMMAR
Nouns in the Subject
Nouns in the Predicate
Words That Signal Nouns
Singular and Plural Nouns
Possessive Nouns
Proper Nouns
Pronouns

COMPOSITION
Making Sentences Grow

MECHANICS
Using Capital Letters
Writing Plurals and
Possessives

VOCABULARY
Exact Nouns
Compound Words

USAGE
Using *a* or *an*

In this unit, you will work with words that name persons, places, things, and ideas. You will also work with words that substitute for nouns.

1 What Are Nouns?

You know what words are. But do you know what words do? Different kinds of words do different things. Some words show action. Some words describe. Some words name. What do the underlined words in the following sentence do?

The <u>girl</u> went to the <u>farm</u> on a <u>bus</u>.

The underlined words name. What are words that name called? Which noun in the sentence names a person? Which noun names a place? Which noun names a thing?

Words that name are called *nouns*. Nouns name persons, places, and things.

Exercise A

Find the nouns in the sentences below. Tell whether each noun you find names a person, a place, or a thing.

1. My mother bought a watch in the city.
2. A turtle crawled across the road.
3. Some birds build nests with mud.
4. The taxi pulled up to the curb.
5. An apple fell from the tree.

Exercise B

Read each sentence. For each box, use a noun that names a person, place, or thing.

1. The ☐ turned off the ☐ in the ☐.
2. My ☐ climbed the ☐ in two ☐.
3. The ☐ raced past the ☐.
4. The ☐ of ☐ scared the ☐.
5. My ☐ works near the ☐.

Exercise C

Write these sentences:

1. In sentence 1, use only nouns that name persons.
2. In sentence 2, use only nouns that name places.
3. In sentence 3, use only nouns that name things.

Exercise D

Pretend that you are on the bus pictured on pages 54–55. Name different kinds of people you can see on the bus. Name some places the bus will probably pass. Name some things you can see from the window of the bus. Name some things you can see when you look at the bus from the outside. Are all the persons, places, and things you named nouns?

57

Nouns in the Subject

When you use words, you usually use them in sentences. Different kinds of words are used in different ways in a sentence. How are nouns used in a sentence?

The old rake / was rusty.

What is the subject of this sentence? What is the key word in the subject? What kind of word is *rake?*

The key word in the subject is often a noun.

Exercise A

Write each sentence below. Draw a slash mark between the subject and the predicate. Then draw a line under the noun that is the key word in the subject.

1. A building was burning.
2. A woman pulled the alarm.
3. An engine roared down the street.
4. The firefighters put out the fire.
5. The street was busy.

Exercise B

Tell whether each noun you underlined for Exercise A names a person, a place, or a thing.

Nouns in the Predicate 3

Look at the underlined word in this sentence:

The firefighter / climbed the <u>ladder</u>.

What is the subject of the sentence? What is the predicate? What kind of word is <u>ladder</u>?

A noun is often used in the predicate of a sentence.

Exercise

Write each sentence below. Draw a line under each key word in the subject. Circle each noun in the predicate.

1. The girl walked the dog.
2. A tornado damaged the barn.
3. The owner opened the door.
4. A pin can break a balloon.
5. The child knew the answer.
6. The truck crossed the bridge.
7. The farmer grows potatoes.
8. The mower cut the grass evenly.
9. My brother had a party.
10. The parents served sandwiches.
11. The doctor saved my life.
12. The child brushed her teeth.

4 Words That Signal Nouns

Some words signal other words. Look at the underlined words in this sentence:

I found <u>a</u> feather from <u>an</u> eagle on <u>the</u> ground.

The words *a*, *an*, and *the* are articles. What word follows *a*? What word follows *an*? What word follows *the*? What kind of words are *feather*, *eagle*, and *ground*?

The articles *a*, *an*, and *the* signal nouns.

Read this sentence:

The small brown cat likes mice.

What noun does the article *The* signal? Does the noun *cat* come right after the article? Find the noun in the predicate. Does *mice* have an article before it?

Sometimes one or more words come between an article and a noun. Sometimes a noun has no article before it.

 **Exercise**

Circle the articles in the following sentences. Draw a line under the noun each article signals.

1. The clock made a loud noise.
2. A tall man walked out of the house.
3. A balloon floated in the sky.
4. The boat landed on an island.
5. The president waved a small blue flag.

One or More Than One? 5

Look at the underlined words in this sentence:

The <u>boy</u> picked up the <u>stick</u>.

How many do you think of when you see the noun *boy*? How many do you think of when you see the noun *stick*? What is a noun that names one person or thing called?

A noun that names one person, place, or thing is called a *singular noun*.

Now look at the underlined words in this sentence:

The <u>boys</u> picked up the <u>sticks</u>.

How many do you think of when you see the noun *boys*? How many do you think of when you see the noun *sticks*? What is a noun that names more than one person or thing called?

A noun that names more than one person, place, or thing is called a *plural noun*.

Exercise

Think of a noun for each picture on this page. Tell whether each noun you think of is singular or plural.

6 Adding -s

How do you make a singular noun plural? Nouns form their plurals in different ways. Look at the pairs of nouns below.

1. boy   boys
2. stick   sticks

What letter was added to the singular noun *boy* to make the plural noun *boys?* What letter was added to the singular noun *stick* to make the plural noun *sticks?*

Most nouns form the plural by adding *s* to the singular.

Exercise A

Write the plural form of each of the following singular nouns:

1. word   6. horse
2. home   7. nest
3. fire   8. pack
4. thing   9. letter
5. pie   10. castle

Exercise B

Choose five singular nouns from Exercise A. Use each noun in a sentence. Then write sentences using the plural forms of the same five nouns.

Some nouns do not form their plurals by adding -s. Look at the pairs of nouns below.

1. dress   dresses
2. buzz   buzzes
3. box   boxes
4. wish   wishes
5. inch   inches

With what letters do the singular nouns end? How do nouns ending in *s, x, z, sh,* and *ch* form their plurals?

Most nouns that end in *s, x, z, sh,* and *ch* form the plural by adding *-es* to the singular.

Exercise A

Write the plural form of each of the following singular nouns:

1. bush
2. lunch
3. tax
4. dish
5. grass
6. mix
7. fizz
8. witch

Exercise B

Choose five singular nouns from Exercise A. Use each noun in a sentence. Then write sentences using the plural forms of the same five nouns.

8 Possessive Nouns

Read this sentence:

My brother found the dog's leash.

Which word in the sentence shows that the dog has something? What is a noun like *dog's* called?

A noun that shows who or what has or owns something is called a *possessive noun.*

Look at the sentence again. What mark and what letter were added to the singular noun *dog* to make the possessive noun *dog's?*

Singular nouns form the possessive by adding an apostrophe followed by an *s*.

Exercise

Write each sentence below. Use the possessive form of the noun on the left for the box.

friend's   **1.** I saw my ☐ name in the paper.
book   **2.** What is that ☐ title?
aunt   **3.** My ☐ new job is exciting.
teacher   **4.** Did you see the ☐ new bike?
mayor   **5.** The ☐ speech was on TV.
cat   **6.** I filled the ☐ bowl with water.
cow   **7.** Butter is made from ☐ milk.
flower   **8.** The ☐ petals drooped.

More About Possessive Nouns

Read the sentences below. How is the possessive noun in sentence 1 different from the possessive noun in sentence 2?

1. The pupil's books are on the shelf.
2. The pupils' books are on the shelf.

In sentence 1, the possessive noun *pupil's* is singular. In sentence 2, the possessive noun *pupils'* is plural. In sentence 2, the books belong to more than one pupil. How do plural nouns ending in *s* form the possessive?

Plural nouns ending in *s* form the possessive by adding an apostrophe only.

CAREER CLUES

Do you like cartoons? You can read my cartoons in the newspaper. I am a _____.

Exercise

Write each sentence. Use the possessive form of the noun on the left for the box.

birds	**1.** We saw three ☐ nests.
clowns	**2.** The ☐ hats fell on the floor.
friends	**3.** I keep my ☐ addresses in a book.
pupils	**4.** The teacher called the ☐ names.
neighbors	**5.** Our ☐ trees are huge.
workers	**6.** The ☐ hands were scarred.
lions	**7.** Stay away from the ☐ cage.
girls	**8.** The ☐ team won the race.

MORE PRACTICE

A. Write the plural form of each of these nouns:

1. book
2. lunch
3. patch
4. month
5. glass
6. bunch
7. word
8. sign
9. boat
10. cake
11. animal
12. dish
13. sense
14. color
15. beach
16. lace
17. chance
18. shoe
19. pass
20. wax

B. Copy the following sentences. Make each noun ending in ☐ show ownership. If the noun is singular, put *S* after your sentence. If it is plural, put *P* after your sentence.

1. We have been learning about our parents☐ jobs.
2. A baker☐ day begins very early.
3. Ranchers☐ horses must be well trained.
4. A farmer☐ job is harder in the summer.
5. The nurse☐ work may be done at night.
6. Storekeepers☐ goods must be neat and clean.
7. Telephone operators☐ voices must be pleasing.
8. Books are the teacher☐ tools.
9. A cook☐ food must be good.
10. The doctor☐ job is to keep us well.
11. Writers☐ books must be interesting.
12. A diver☐ work is exciting.
13. An artist☐ eyes must be keen.
14. Miners☐ jobs take them under the earth.
15. Pilots☐ jobs take them above the earth.

66

Proper Nouns 10

Read the sentences below. How are the underlined nouns different in each sentence?

1. A boy went to a city one day.
2. Stan went to Dallas on Tuesday.

In which sentence do the nouns name an exact person, place, and thing? What are nouns like *Stan, Dallas,* and *Tuesday* called? With what kind of letter does a proper noun begin?

A noun that names an exact person, place, or thing is called a *proper noun.* A proper noun begins with a capital letter.

Remember to use capital letters to begin:

1. The exact names of persons and pets
2. The exact names of towns, cities, and states
3. The exact names of months
4. The exact names of days of the week, holidays, and special days

Facts About Language

Where do place names come from? Some places were named for their location: *Edgewater, Bridgewater.* Some were named after people: *Lincoln,* Nebraska; *Houston* (Texas).

Exercise

Write the pairs of nouns below. Use a capital letter to begin each proper noun.

1. holiday — halloween
2. monday — day
3. month — march
4. texas — state
5. friend — terese
6. city — miami

11 More About Proper Nouns

Look at the underlined words in the following sentences.

1. I helped my <u>mother</u> rake the lawn.
2. I helped <u>Mother</u> rake the lawn.

How are these two sentences different? Why does *Mother* begin with a capital letter in sentence 2?

When a word like *Mother* or *Father* is used as a person's name, it is a proper noun. It begins with a capital letter.

 Exercise A

Write these sentences correctly.

1. Is mother home from work yet?
2. We gave father a new watch.
3. My Dad likes to wash the dishes.

How do proper nouns form the possessive?

My friend Pete's glove is in Mother's car.

Most proper nouns form the possessive by adding an apostrophe and an *s*.

 Exercise B

Write the possessive form of each proper noun.

1. Ethel   2. Hawaii   3. Spot   4. Clyde   5. Dad

MORE PRACTICE

A. Write each sentence. For the box, use one of the proper nouns at the left.

Sally

Bridgeport

Rusty

Christmas

Wednesday

1. Mom and I went away last ☐.

2. We visited Aunt ☐.

3. She has a dog named ☐.

4. He was born on ☐.

5. He is the nicest dog in ☐.

B. Write the sentences below. Use capital letters where they belong.

1. we saw mary and jack last tuesday.

2. every hanukkah we visit grandpa in florida.

3. my dog's name is spike.

4. in march pedro will be nine years old.

C. Write a proper noun for each of the nouns below. Use each proper noun in a sentence.

1. city   **3.** boy   **5.** month   **7.** girl   **9.** town

2. day   **4.** horse   **6.** state   **8.** dog   **10.** holiday

D. Write the sentences below. Begin the words *mother* and *father* with a capital letter when they are used as someone's name.

1. My mother drives to work.

2. I asked dad to help me build a racer.

3. He said to ask mother for help.

4. When mother came home, I asked her.

69

12 Pronouns

What do you call someone who takes the place of someone else? Read the following story to find the answer.

1. Angelo was supposed to be in the class play, but he got sick.
2. Ms. Horton had to get someone else to take his place.
3. She asked Donald if he would be Angelo's substitute.
4. Donald said he would be glad to take Angelo's place.

Some words can also substitute for other words. What word in sentence 1 is a substitute for the noun *Angelo?* What word in sentence 3 is a substitute for the noun *Ms. Horton?* Words like *he* and *she* are pronouns.

A pronoun is a word that substitutes for a noun.

Exercise A

Find the pronouns in the following story. Name the noun each pronoun substitutes for.

1. Karen asked Bill if he would help her.
2. She had to take her cats to the vet.
3. They were going for their annual checkup.
4. She wanted him to take them on his bike.
5. But he told her that it was broken.

The following chart will help you to use pronouns correctly.

WHEN YOU SUBSTITUTE A PRONOUN FOR . . .	USE THE PRONOUNS . . .
1. yourself	I, me, my, mine
2. yourself with others	we, us, our, ours
3. a girl or a woman	she, her, hers
4. a boy or a man	he, him, his
5. one thing	it, its
6. more than one person or thing	they, them, their, theirs

Exercise B

Write the following sentences. Use a pronoun that makes sense for each box.

1. Mary helped ☐ father wash the car.
2. Is that your pen or ☐?
3. The elm trees lost ☐ leaves.
4. Where should we have ☐ party?
5. Alec said that ☐ would be late.
6. ☐ gave our parents a surprise party.
7. The neighbors helped ☐ cut down our tree.

13 Writing Sentences with Pronouns

How do pronouns help you to write better sentences? If there were no pronouns, you would have to repeat nouns over and over again. Read this story:

Arlene was in <u>Arlene's</u> room. <u>Arlene</u> was reading a book about magic. <u>The book</u> was so interesting, that <u>Arlene</u> didn't hear <u>Arlene's</u> brother Marty come into <u>Arlene's</u> room. Marty sneaked up behind <u>Arlene</u>. <u>Marty</u> looked over <u>Arlene's</u> shoulder to see what <u>Arlene</u> was reading. Then <u>Marty</u> touched Arlene and ran out. Arlene jumped out of <u>Arlene's</u> chair. But when <u>Arlene</u> turned around, no one was there.

Read the story again. This time use pronouns for the underlined words. Which story sounds better?

 Exercise

Write the following sentences. Use pronouns in place of the underlined words.

1. Nick grabbed <u>Nick's</u> coat as <u>Nick</u> ran out of the house.
2. Clara was waiting outside for <u>Nick</u> on <u>Clara's</u> bike.
3. <u>Nick and Clara</u> were going to see <u>Clara's</u> parents' new boat.
4. <u>The new boat</u> is a sailboat.
5. <u>The new boat's</u> sails are red and white.

Making Sentences Grow

When you see an article in a sentence, you know that a noun will follow. The noun often comes right after the article. Look at the article and noun in the subject of this sentence:

The dog barked at the cat.

You can make a sentence grow by adding one or more words that tell about or describe the noun. These describing words usually come between the article and the noun.

The small brown dog barked.

You can also use words to tell about or describe a noun in the predicate of a sentence.

The dog barked at the fat gray cat.

Exercise

Write the following sentences. Use at least one describing word before each noun.

1. A kite floated in the sky.
2. We live in a house.
3. The snake hissed at a duck.
4. Vinnie made a cake.
5. The boat rocked in the water.
6. I read a story about a horse.
7. The food was on a table.
8. Did you see the train?

15 Working with Words

Fun with Nouns

Here are four ways to tell whether a word is a noun.

1. Nouns name persons, places, and things.
2. A noun is often the key word in the subject.
3. The words *a, an,* and *the* tell that a noun will follow.
4. Nouns have a plural form and a possessive form.

Remember these four clues as you play the game in Exercise A.

 Exercise A

The sentences below are in a made-up language. Write the sentences and underline the nouns.

1. The nerd neeped.
2. Foofs fozzle.
3. The boff's binks boffled.
4. The clugs clombled.
5. A mip's mep mipped.
6. An off uffed.

Exercise B

Make up sentences like those in Exercise A. Exchange papers with a partner.

What do you call a book that helps someone cook? What do you call a coat that you wear in the rain? What are words like *cookbook* and *raincoat* called?

A word made by putting two or more words together is called a *compound word.*

Compound Words

Exercise C

Write the sentences below. Use a compound word for each box.

1. A drop made of rain is a ☐.
2. A ball made of snow is a ☐.
3. A ball that is thrown through a basket is a ☐.
4. A cage for a bird is a ☐.
5. A hook used for catching fish is a ☐.
6. A house with a light on top is a ☐.
7. The room in which a bed is kept is a ☐.
8. The yard of a church is a ☐.
9. A room in a school is a ☐.
10. A ship that flies through space is a ☐.

Exercise D

Write a compound word for each picture on this page. What word is part of all three compound words? How do compound words help make your language grow?

75

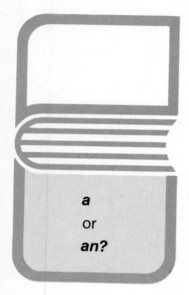

a
or
an?

How do you know when to use the articles *a* and *an?* Read aloud the words in each of these groups:

1		2	
an apple	an orange	a boat	a table
an eagle	an uncle	a flower	a woman
an island		a house	

Look at the nouns in group 1. Is *a* or *an* used before each noun? With what letters do the words begin? The letters *a, e, i, o,* and *u* are vowels. Words that begin with these letters usually begin with a vowel sound.

Use *an* before a noun that begins with a vowel sound.

All the other letters of the alphabet are consonants. With what kind of letters do the nouns in group 2 begin? Words that begin with consonant letters usually begin with a consonant sound. Is *a* or *an* used before each noun in group 2?

Use *a* before a noun that begins with a consonant sound.

When you use a describing word between an article and a noun, you may have to change the article. Look at the following sentences.

1. I had a pencil and an eraser.
2. I had an old pencil and a new eraser.

Why did the articles change in the second sentence?

Use *an* before any word that begins with a vowel sound. Use *a* before any word that begins with a consonant sound.

Exercise A

Write the following sentences. Use *a* or *an* for each box.

1. ☐ ape swung from ☐ tree.
2. I saw ☐ clown on ☐ elephant.
3. She put ☐ olive in ☐ jar.
4. I have ☐ idea for ☐ story.

Exercise B

Write the following sentences. Use *a* or *an* for each box.

1. I have ☐ necklace from Arizona.
2. I have ☐ Indian necklace from Arizona.
3. She gave me ☐ apricot.
4. She gave me ☐ dried apricot.
5. It was ☐ easy test.
6. It was ☐ hard test.
7. We watched the ants build ☐ anthill.
8. We watched the ants build ☐ big anthill.
9. ☐ usher took us to our seats.
10. ☐ young usher took us to our seats.

On pages 22–23, you were asked to write sentences that give clear pictures. One way to give a clear picture is to use exact nouns. In the editing exercises that follow, you will edit someone else's work. Remember to edit your own sentences for exact nouns.

A. Write the following sentences. Cross out each underlined noun. Write an exact noun for each word you cross out.

1. The <u>man</u> made a cake.
2. I got a book from the <u>building</u>.
3. Where did you buy that <u>thing</u>?
4. She got a <u>present</u> for her birthday.
5. Do you like to chew <u>stuff</u>?
6. That <u>boy</u> has a good voice.

B. Edit the story below. Think of a more exact noun for each underlined noun. Then write the story, using the more exact nouns.

Visiting the Airport

Yesterday our <u>group</u> visited the <u>place</u>. While we were standing there, we saw many <u>things</u>. A <u>person</u> told us how she flies the <u>thing</u>. We asked her many <u>things</u> which she answered. On the way home, we stopped at a <u>place</u> and bought cold <u>drinks</u>. All of us enjoyed the <u>thing</u> and we hope we go on another <u>thing</u> soon.

EDITING EXERCISE

Reviewing Your Skills

The page numerals after each heading show you where to look if you need help with this review.

Finding Nouns in the Subject and the Predicate (58–59)

Write each sentence below. Draw a slash mark between the subject and the predicate. Then circle each noun you find in the subject and the predicate.

1. The girl built an airplane.
2. The children saw an elephant.
3. A robin built that nest.
4. The principal has a red telephone.

Finding Noun Signals (60)

Write each sentence below. Circle each article. Draw a line under the noun the article signals.

1. The hikers climbed the hill.
2. The newspaper is in the mailbox.
3. A cat sat on the fence.
4. The earthquake shook the buildings.

Writing Plural Nouns (61–63)

Write the plural form of each of the following singular nouns:

1. pen
2. box
3. couch
4. chair
5. brush
6. chicken
7. dish
8. car

Writing Possessive Nouns (64–65)

Write each sentence below. Use the possessive form of the noun on the left for the box in each sentence.

(cousin)   **1.** My ☐ apartment is below ours.

(dog)   **2.** That old slipper is my ☐ favorite toy.

(principal) **3.** The ☐ speech was short.

(aunt)   **4.** My ☐ fishing line tangled with mine.

Recognizing Proper Nouns (67)

Write the pairs of nouns below. Use a capital letter to begin each proper noun.

1. dog – lassie   **3.** june – month   **5.** horse – misty

2. city – dallas   **4.** day – friday   **6.** manuel – friend

Using Pronouns (70–72)

Write each sentence. Use pronouns in place of the underlined words.

1. Mr. Moore had left <u>Mr. Moore's</u> car lights on.

2. <u>Mr. Moore's</u> son ran outside to turn <u>the lights</u> off.

3. The cat's collar has bells on <u>the collar</u>.

4. <u>The bells</u> warn birds that the cat is near.

Making Sentences Grow (73)

Write each sentence. Use at least one describing word before each noun.

1. The <u>cabin</u> stood on a <u>hill</u>.

2. A <u>bike</u> leaned against the <u>fence</u>.

Testing Your Skills

Finding Nouns in the Subject and the Predicate

Write each sentence below. Draw a slash mark between the subject and the predicate. Then circle each noun you find in the subject and the predicate.

1. Two sandwiches filled the bag.
2. The farmer plowed the field.
3. Two tractors are making that noise.
4. An otter caught a fish.
5. A carpenter fixed the shelf.
6. Robins have built a nest.

Finding Noun Signals

Write each sentence below. Circle each article. Draw a line under the noun the article signals.

1. The doctor look at the chart.
2. A small child peered through the window.
3. The coach locks up the equipment.
4. The car needs a new battery.
5. The smoke set off an alarm.
6. The firefighters rushed to the scene.

Writing Plural Nouns

Write the plural form of each of the following singular nouns:

1. fox
2. branch
3. wish
4. patch
5. ranch
6. lunch
7. chair
8. dime

Writing Possessive Nouns

Write each sentence below. Use the possessive form of the noun at the left for the box in each sentence.

(sister)   **1.** I often ride my ☐ bike.

(cat)   **2.** The dog ate the ☐ food.

(doctor)   **3.** The ☐ office is on Maple Avenue.

(parrot)   **4.** The ☐ cage was open.

Recognizing Proper Nouns

Write these sentences correctly:

1. When is aunt mae moving to florida?

2. Help dad move the couch.

3. Is mom working late tonight?

4. A neighbor gave father a ride home.

Using Pronouns

Write each sentence. Use pronouns in place of the underlined words.

1. Charlie stubbed Charlie's toe on Charlie's dresser.

2. The smock had spots of paint on the smock.

3. Claire and her friend are planning a picnic.

4. Dotty's dog ran off with Dotty's tennis shoe.

Making Sentences Grow

Write each sentence. Use at least one describing word before each noun.

1. The boy carried a box.

2. The mechanic fixed the car.

82

Skills Checkup

Putting Words in Order (10–11)

Change the order of the words in each group below to make a sentence.

1. the told a funny girl story
2. purred kitten the softly
3. my painted her room sister
4. someone door the slammed

Using Capital Letters and Punctuation Marks (17–20)

Write each sentence. Use capital letters where they are needed. Use a period or a question mark at the end.

1. i have a new bike
2. would you like to ride it
3. my dog prince follows me
4. does rags follow you

Writing Titles (41)

Write these titles correctly:

1. on a bike hike
2. a day at the beach
3. lost in the city
4. the sounds of summer
5. a surprise party
6. alone on the stage

Showing That Someone Is Speaking (42–43)

Write the sentences below. Use commas, capital letters, and quotation marks to show that someone is speaking.

1. pat asked what is full of holes but can hold water
2. jerry replied i don't know
3. pat answered it is a sponge

Friendly Letters

COMPOSITION
Writing a Friendly Letter
Addressing an Envelope
Writing a Postcard

MECHANICS
Using Commas in Friendly Letters
Using a Period After an Abbreviation
Using Capital Letters

USAGE
Using *any* or *no; them* or *those*

In this unit, you will study the parts of a friendly letter. You will also learn how to address an envelope and send a postcard. Then you will meet someone called Hulla-Baloo, who celebrates a birthday in a most unusual way.

1 Kinds of Letters

James wrote this letter to Shirley:

> *33 Charles Street*
> *New York City, New York 10003*
> *March 26, 19--*

Dear Shirley,

> *My birthday is on Saturday, April 4. Instead of having a party, I am asking some friends to visit the Museum of Natural History with my aunt and me.*
> *I hope you can come. Please let me know by April 1. We will meet at my house at 9 o'clock.*

> *Your friend,*
> *James*

Shirley wrote this letter back:

> *45-05 178 Street*
> *Flushing, New York 11358*
> *March 29, 19--*

Dear James,

> *Thank you for asking me to help celebrate your birthday. I will be at your house at 9 o'clock on April 4.*

> *Your friend,*
> *Shirley*

After the trip to the museum, Shirley wrote James a note to thank him for asking her. Then she wrote a letter to her best friend in Chicago. She told her about the museum trip and everything else that happened that week.

Why do people write letters? What kind of letter did James write? What kinds of letters did Shirley write? Invitations, thank-you notes, and newsy letters are friendly letters.

Exercise A

Talk about the sentences below. They will help you discover some guides for writing a friendly letter.

1. Mark's letters are boring. He never tells you anything interesting.
2. You can never read Clara's letters. Her writing is messy and hard to read.
3. I don't bother about using capital letters and punctuation marks. They don't make any difference, do they?

Exercise B

Pretend that you were with Shirley and James when they visited the museum pictured on pages 84–85. What would you write to a friend about the trip? Would you tell only about the museum? Or would you tell about James's birthday?

2 Parts of a Friendly Letter

A friendly letter has five parts. Each part has its own place in the letter. Each part has its own job to do.

Exercise A

Read the letter on the next page. Then answer the following questions.

1. Where is the heading? What does it tell?
2. Where is the greeting? What person's name is used in the greeting?
3. What does the body tell?
4. Where is the closing? What does it tell?
5. Where is the signature? What is another word for *signature?*

Look again at the letter on the next page. Where do you see empty spaces? These spaces are called margins. There are margins at the top and bottom of the page and on both sides.

Exercise B

Look at the left margin of the letter on the next page. Then answer the following questions.

1. Where does the greeting begin?
2. Where do most of the lines in the body of the letter begin?

1215 Hamilton Road
Lake City, Florida 32055
July 14, 19__

Dear Chris,

You won't believe what happened yesterday at the beach. It was hot and crowded. The water was wonderful, and I was having a great time.

All of a sudden I heard a loud siren. Everyone got out of the water in a hurry. I didn't know what was happening. Then someone told me there was a shark in the water. It was kind of scary. I didn't see the shark, but I didn't go back in the water either.

Tomorrow we're going to have a picnic.

Your best friend,
Marge

3 The Heading

Talk about the answers to these questions about the heading in the letter on page 89:

1. What do the first two lines of the heading tell? If Marge lived in the country, the first line of her address might read "R.R. 3." *R.R.* stands for *Rural Route*. If Marge's mail were delivered to a box in the post office, the first line of her address might read "P.O. Box 62." What does *P.O.* stand for?
2. What is the numeral at the end of the second line? Do you know what your ZIP code is?
3. What does the last line of the heading tell?
4. Where are capital letters used in the heading? Where are commas used?

Follow these guidelines for writing a heading:

1. Place the heading near the upper right corner.

2. Use capital letters for:
   a. Names of streets, avenues, and roads
   b. *Rural Route* and *Post Office Box*
   c. The short forms, *R.R.* and *P.O. Box*
   d. Names of towns, cities, and states
   e. Names of months

3. Use a comma between:
   a. The name of the town or city and the name of the state
   b. The day and the year

4. Use periods with *R.R.* and *P.O.*

Exercise A

Write some addresses you know. Then write some make-believe addresses. Make up a date for each address. Write each address and date as the heading of a letter.

Exercise B

Write these headings correctly. Use the guidelines for capital letters.

1. 6 hilltop road
   san mateo, california 94402
   june 13, 19--

2. 9002 muldoon road
   bath, indiana 47010
   october 2, 19--

3. r.r.6
   ocracoke, north carolina 27960
   march 21, 19--

Exercise C

Write these headings correctly. Use the guidelines for capital letters, commas, and periods.

1. 426 west fifth street
   topeka, kansas 66605
   april 11 19--

2. p o box 6412
   granger wyoming 82934
   december 24 19--

3. 13 harmony lane
   rutland vermont 05701
   august 4 19--

4 The Greeting

Look again at the letter on page 89. Where is the greeting? Which words are written with capital letters? What mark of punctuation follows the greeting? Now look at the greetings below. Pay special attention to the second word in each greeting.

1. Dear Uncle Nick,   3. Dear Ms. Bellows,
2. Dear Miss Coburn,   4. Dear Dr. Randall,

The words *Uncle, Miss, Ms.,* and *Dr.* are titles. A short form of a word is called an *abbreviation.* Which of the titles are abbreviations? What mark follows an abbreviation?

Follow these guidelines for writing a greeting:

1. Write the greeting at the left margin. Leave a space below the heading.

2. Use capital letters for:
   a. The first word of a greeting
   b. The name of a person
   c. A title such as *Mr., Mrs., Ms.,* and *Dr.*

3. Use a period after an abbreviation like *Dr.*

4. Use a comma after the greeting.

 Exercise

Write these greetings correctly.

1. dear aunt mary 2. dear mrs blake

92

Look at the letter on page 89. What is the main part of the letter?

Look at the left-hand margin of the letter on page 89. Where does the first line of writing in the body begin? Find two more lines that are indented.

The body of a friendly letter is made up of sentences. How should each sentence begin? What kind of mark comes after each sentence?

What did Marge write about in her letter? Do you think Chris liked reading about the shark?

Follow these guidelines when you write the body of a friendly letter:

1. Indent the first line.

2. Indent whenever you begin to write about a new idea.

3. Begin each sentence with a capital letter and end it with a period or another mark.

4. Write about something interesting.

Exercise

Write this body of a letter correctly:

i hope you are enjoying the beach it is raining here again today bobbie and i played checkers for a while then we made a cake now we are waiting for it to cool then we will ice it and eat it when are you coming to visit us

The Closing and the Signature

Here is the closing of the letter on page 89. Which word begins with a capital letter? What mark follows the closing?

Your best friend,

Here is the signature for the letter on page 89. What kind of noun is the signature? How does it begin? Is there any mark after the signature?

Marge

Now look at the heading, the closing, and the signature in the letter on page 89. Are these three parts of a friendly letter all in a line?

Follow these guidelines for writing the closing and the signature:

1. Write the closing under the last line of the body in line with the heading.

2. Begin the first word of the closing with a capital letter.

3. Use a comma after the closing.

4. Write your signature in line with the closing.

5. Write your name clearly.

Exercise

Write these closings and signatures correctly.

1. your brother
henry
2. your niece
caroline
3. yours truly
frances healy
4. sincerely
donald brent
5. your friend
theresa

6. love
carmen
7. stay well
juan
8. your best pal
oscar
9. thank you
gloria gates
10. your cousin
elizabeth

MORE PRACTICE

Name the following parts of a friendly letter. Then put the five parts in order. Write them correctly as parts of the same letter.

1. your friend
2. 2886 briggs avenue
detroit michigan 48211
november 17 19__
3. jessica
4. did you hear what happened on our block last week a water main broke and made a big hole in the middle of the street many basements flooded now we have a small lake on our block i wish you were here to see it
5. dear marilou

7 Addressing the Envelope

An envelope is a package that carries your letter through the mail. The envelope tells who sent the letter and where it is going. The ZIP code helps the post office deliver the mail.

Look at the following envelope. Then read the guidelines below.

RETURN ADDRESS

William Marston
36 Bethune Street
New York, New York 10014

ADDRESS

Miss Cathy Dawson
399 Pecos Street
Denver, Colorado 80223

1. Write the return address in the upper left corner of the envelope.

2. Start the address in the middle of the envelope.

3. Use ZIP codes in the return address and the address.

Exercise

Draw your own envelope and address it to a friend.

Writing and Mailing a Letter

Most friendly letters are newsy letters. In a newsy letter, you usually write about things that happened to you, your family, or your friends. The things you write about should also be interesting to the person to whom you are writing.

Exercise A

Follow these steps for writing and mailing a friendly letter.

1. Think of someone you want to write a letter to.
2. Decide what you want to write about. Make sure that the person you're writing to will be interested in your news.
3. Write the letter. Make sure you write all the parts correctly and in order. Also make sure that your writing is neat and clear.
4. Address the envelope. Don't forget the ZIP codes. Seal the envelope and put a stamp on it.
5. Mail the letter. Then wait for a letter from the person you wrote to.

CAREER CLUES

I bring you birthday cards and other kinds of written messages. I am a _____.

Exercise B

Cut out a picture from a newspaper or magazine. The picture should show something happening. Then write a letter to a friend about the picture.

⑨ Writing Better Letters

AL

You should know how to spell all the words you write in a letter. You should also know which words begin with capital letters.

Every heading in a friendly letter has the name of a month in it. How do the names of the months begin? Can you spell the names of all twelve months?

NY

Exercise A

Write the letters in each group below in the correct order to spell the name of a month. Remember to begin each name with a capital letter.

1. gaustu
2. ceborot
3. anujray
4. ejnu

5. venomber
6. pilar
7. ramch
8. dremeceb

9. amy
10. stepbreem
11. lyju
12. ufaryber

MN

Can you spell the names of the days of the week? How does each one begin?

Exercise B

Write the names of the days of the week in order. Remember to begin each name with a capital letter.

The Post Office uses special abbreviations for the names of the states. Each one is two capital letters without a period. Some of these state abbreviations are shown on this page.

FL

Exercise C

Match the abbreviations on the left with the names of the states on the right.

1. CA **a.** North Carolina
2. KY **b.** Kentucky
3. PA **c.** South Dakota
4. NC **d.** Georgia
5. AZ **e.** Ohio

6. GA **f.** California
7. SD **g.** New Mexico
8. VT **h.** Vermont
9. OH **i.** Arizona
10. NM **j.** Pennsylvania

You use these words and abbreviations in the greetings and closings of friendly letters. Can you spell them? Do you remember when to write them with a capital letter? Do you remember when to use a period?

mother	grandfather	Mrs.	son
father	uncle	Ms.	daughter
aunt	Mr.	nephew	cousin
grandmother	Miss	niece	friend

Exercise D

Write the following greetings and closings as you would in a letter:

1. dear grandmother
2. dear mr johnson
3. dear aunt bea
4. your son
5. your cousin
6. your pal

99

Read the friendly letter below. What kind of letter is it? Write the letter correctly. Then address the envelope correctly.

13 smithtown road
hazel kentucky 42049
february 6 1980

dear grandma

i got your present in the mail today it's just the kind of paint set i wanted thank you very much i am going to paint a picture and send it to you do you like flowers or birds
love

                                    alice

---

alice myers
13 smithtown road
hazel kentucky 42049

mrs betty holmes
111 willow street
parker idaho 83438

EDITING EXERCISE

Postcards are fun to send when you go on a trip. They are easy to send too. When you send a postcard, you don't need an envelope. You write the address right on the postcard.

Picture postcards have a picture on the front. You write your message and the address on the back. Look at the postcard below.

Dear Tony,
Boston is beautiful. There are many old buildings here. We went to Concord and Lexington yesterday. And tomorrow we are going on a sailboat. I wish you were with us.
Love,
Maria

Mr. Anthony Fiore
1 Christopher Street
New York, NY 10014

Where is the message on the back of the postcard? Where is the address? What part of a friendly letter is missing from the postcard? What part of an envelope is missing?

Exercise

Cut out a 6-inch by 9-inch piece of paper. Draw or paste a picture on one side. Draw a line down the center of the other side. Write a note and address it.

11 Using Your Language

any
or
no?

Read the sentence below. Tell what is wrong with it.

I don't have no money.

The word *don't* stands for the two words *do not*. The word *no* means "not any." How would you say the sentence above correctly?

1. I don't have any money.
2. I have no money.

Both of these sentences mean the same thing. Sentence 1 uses *not*. Sentence 2 uses *no*. Both sentences are correct.

Do not use the words *no* and *not* in the same sentence when only one of them is needed.

Exercise A

Write the following sentences. Use *any* or *no* for the box in each sentence. Remember that *n't* means *not*.

1. They didn't find ☐ flowers.
2. I saw ☐ mushrooms.
3. Jay can't eat ☐ spinach.
4. He won't drink ☐ tea.
5. Don't tell me ☐ lies.

Exercise B

Write the following sentences correctly. You can write some sentences in two correct ways.

1. Ella doesn't want no popcorn.
2. I'm not going to sing no songs.
3. I didn't see no ghosts.
4. We don't have no bananas.
5. Franco won't eat no lemons.

People sometimes mix up the words *them* and *those*. Look at the underlined words in the following sentences:

1. I didn't take <u>those</u> books.
2. I didn't take <u>them</u>.

What kind of word follows the underlined word in sentence 1?

them
or
those?

Those can be used to signal a noun.
Them is never used to signal a noun.

Exercise C

Write the following sentences. Use *those* or *them* for the box in each sentence.

1. Don't wake up ☐ bees.
2. The goat ate all ☐ flowers.
3. I hope he enjoyed ☐.
4. ☐ frogs are driving me crazy.
5. I like ☐ birds.

On pages 86–87, you read about James, who celebrated his birthday with a trip to a museum. Now you will read about Prince Hulla-Baloo, who celebrates his birthday in a most unusual way. Then in Lesson 12, you will stretch your imagination by becoming part of Hulla-Baloo's world.

The LOUDEST Noise in the World

Once upon a time, the noisiest place in the world was a city called Hub-Bub. The people of Hub-Bub never talked, they yelled. They were very proud that their ducks were the quackiest, their doors the slammiest, and their police whistles the shrillest in the whole world.

Of all the noisy people in Hub-Bub, the noisiest was a young Prince named Hulla-Baloo. He could make more noise than the grown-ups. Hulla-Baloo loved to yell, bang pots and pans together and blow a whistle, all at the same time.

His favorite game was to climb up a ladder, piling up trash cans and tin pails as high as he could, and then—knock over the whole pile with a loud crash. He used to make the piles higher and higher, and they made louder and louder crashes. But still he wasn't satisfied. Prince Hulla-Baloo wanted to hear the loudest noise in the world.

STRETCHING

A few weeks before the Prince's birthday his father, the King of Hub-Bub, asked him what he wanted for a birthday present. "Well," answered Prince Hulla-Baloo, "I'll tell you what I've been wanting for a long time. I want to hear every person in the world yell at the same minute. If millions and millions of people all yelled together, I'm sure that would be the loudest noise in the world."

The more the King considered this idea, the better he liked it. It might be fun, he thought. "Yes, I'll try it," said the King.

So the King got busy. He sent out hundreds of messengers to visit every country, from the hottest jungles to the coldest icelands. Every day thousands of messages were carried—by telegraph and tom-tom, by car and carrier pigeon, by airplane and dog sled. Everyone was delighted with the idea and all would be glad to help. All the people of the world agreed to yell "Happy Birthday" at the same exact time.

YOUR IMAGINATION

Then one afternoon, a lady in a far-away land said to her friend, "What bothers me is how I'm going to hear everyone else yelling when I'm making so much noise myself. All I'll hear is my own voice."

"You're right," answered her friend. "When the time comes, let's open our mouths with the rest of the crowd, but we won't make a sound. Then, while the others are shouting their heads off, we'll be quiet and really hear the noise." Without meaning any harm, the lady told her neighbors about the plan ... and without meaning any harm, they told their neighbors, and so on. Before long, people all over the world, even in the city of Hub-Bub, were privately telling one another to open their mouths at the right time but not to yell, so they would be able to hear all the noise made by everyone else.

And so the important moment came closer and closer. In all corners of the earth crowds of people began gathering in their public meeting places. All over the world eyes stared at large clocks ticking away the seconds. It seemed that a shock of excitement, like electricity, swept around the entire globe. In Hub-Bub, of course, the excitement was especially great.

Thousands of people jammed the palace grounds, cheering and shouting, while high on the balcony the young Prince waited happily for the loudest noise in the world.

Fifteen seconds to go . . . ten seconds . . . five seconds . . . NOW!

Two billion people strained their ears to hear the loudest noise in the world—and two billion people heard nothing but *absolute silence*. Every person had kept quiet so he or she could hear the others yell; every person had expected the others to do the work, while he or she sat back and enjoyed. The people had disappointed Prince Hulla-Baloo. The people of Hub-Bub were particularly ashamed. They hung their heads and began to creep away.

But suddenly they heard a strange sound. It was the Prince, clapping his hands in glee and laughing happily. He was pointing to the garden with great delight. For the first time in his life he was hearing the singing of a little bird, the whispering of the winds in the leaves, the ripple of the water in the brook. For the first time in his life, Prince Hulla-Baloo was hearing the sounds of nature instead of the noise of Hub-Bub. For the first time in his life, the Prince had been given the gift of peace and quiet, and he loved it!

BENJAMIN ELKIN, *The Loudest Noise in the World*

12 Make-Believe Mail

The King of Hub-Bub had to use messengers to tell people around the world of Prince Hulla-Baloo's birthday wish. That was because in those times there was no way to mail letters. Today we can send messages to people by writing them letters. The post office acts as our messenger.

Exercise A

Pretend that you are the King of Hub-Bub. Write a letter to the people of the world. In your letter tell everyone what Prince Hulla-Baloo would like for his birthday. Explain his love of noises and how happy it would make him to hear the loudest noise in the world. Make up a heading, a greeting, a body, a closing, and a signature for your letter.

Exercise B

Now make believe that you are Prince Hulla-Baloo. Write a letter to the people of the world thanking them for your birthday present. Explain why the surprise gift turned out to be much better than the gift you asked for. Also remember to put in all the important parts of a letter.

Reviewing Your Skills

The page numerals after each heading show you where to look if you need help with this review.

Writing Headings Correctly (90–91)

Write these headings correctly:

1. jefferson school
   newark delaware 19711
   june 7 19--

2. 24 ely place
   edison new jersey 08817
   july 27 19--

3. r r 8
   topeka kansas 66605
   september 15 19--

4. 104 lake crest avenue
   rochester new york 14612
   may 22 19--

Writing Greetings Correctly (92)

Write these greetings correctly:

1. dear rick
2. dear aunt sue
3. dear mr dawson
4. dear dr weinman
5. dear dr winston
6. dear miss mason
7. dear mother
8. dear mrs ashley

Writing Closings Correctly (94–95)

Write these closings correctly:

1. your daughter
2. your friend
3. your chum
4. love always
5. your pen pal
6. with love
7. your grandson
8. your good friend
9. your cousin
10. love

Writing a Friendly Letter (86–96)

Put the five parts of the friendly letter in order. Write them correctly as parts of the same letter.

1. your cousin

2. 5ll court street
   chicago illinois 60611
   october 21 19--

3. marlene

4. taffy had three kittens my friends have taken two of them would you like the last kitten it's almost all white with patches of red let me know if you want it

5. dear janice

Addressing Envelopes (96)

Mr. Rush is sending a letter to Dr. Carson. Draw an envelope. Fill in the return address and the address.

mr j r rush
92 hemlock court
arbington pennsylvania 19001

dr elizabeth c carson
1818 ocean drive
canby oregon 97013

Sending Postcards (101)

Cut out a 6-inch by 9-inch piece of paper. Draw or paste a picture on one side. Draw a line down the center of the other side. Write a note on the left side. Address it on the right side.

Testing Your Skills

Writing Headings Correctly

Write these headings correctly:

1. r r 2
   marion north carolina 28752
   october 26 19--

2. p o box 21
   holbrook new york 11741
   february 23 19--

3. 13 vineyard drive
   stony creek virginia 23882
   january 15 19--

4. 3 pilgrim street
   lexington massachusetts 02173
   november 15 19--

Writing Greetings Correctly

Write these greetings correctly:

1. dear jack
2. dear ms leone
3. dear dr abels
4. dear mrs murphy
5. dear cousin
6. dear aunt ethel
7. dear dad
8. dear mr franklin
9. dear uncle tim
10. dear miss williams

Writing Closings Correctly

Write these closings correctly:

1. your cousin
2. your niece
3. your pal
4. your nephew
5. your daughter
6. your neighbor

Writing a Friendly Letter

Put the five parts of the friendly letter in order. Write them correctly as parts of the same letter.

1. your nephew
2. 2003 north front street
   anderson indiana 46012
   may 2 19--
3. dear aunt bertha
4. the book you sent me is very exciting how did you know i like to read about outer space the pictures help me to understand the story thank you very much for this interesting book
5. george

Addressing Envelopes

Mrs. Jackson is sending a letter to Miss Andersen. Draw an envelope. Fill in the return address and the address.

mrs l v jackson
1412 newsome street
shannon mississippi 38868

miss peggy andersen
666 marshall drive
smithfield kentucky 40068

Sending Postcards

Cut out a 6-inch by 9-inch piece of paper. Draw or paste a picture on one side. Draw a line down the center of the other side. Write a note on the left side. Address it on the right side.

Writing Sentences Correctly (17–18)

Write these two kinds of sentences correctly:

1. can you write a friendly letter

2. billy came to see us yesterday

3. did andrea find her mitt

4. mom gave me a new pen

5. what happened to your other pen

6. the letter carrier came very early this morning

Showing That Someone Is Speaking (42–43)

Write the sentences below. Use commas, capital letters, and quotation marks to show that someone is speaking.

1. mother asked what is this in the freezer

2. jill explained that's a snowball

3. mother asked why are you saving it

4. jill said i'm saving it for this summer

5. richard said let me use it as an ice cube

Writing Plural Nouns (62–63)

Write the plural form of each of the following singular nouns:

1. pitch   **6.** brush

2. game   **7.** class

3. rich   **8.** address

4. circus   **9.** cage

5. scratch   **10.** brush

Using the Dictionary

DICTIONARY SKILLS   Alphabetical Order
Entry Words
Guide Words
Meaning

STUDY SKILLS   The Index
The Table of Contents

USAGE   Review

In this unit, you will explore the different kinds of information that can be found in a dictionary. You will also see how poets use words in a very special way.

Looking It Up

Hector was reading a book out loud and Brenda was listening. It was a history book about the ancient countries of Africa. Then Hector read this sentence.

An obelisk stood on either side of the temple door.

"What's an obelisk?" asked Brenda.

"I don't know," said Hector. "I think it's some kind of guard dog."

"No," said Brenda, "I think it must be a special kind of tree."

Just then Hector's mother walked into the room.

"Mom," said Hector, "what's an obelisk?"

"Why don't you look it up?" she said.

"That's right," said Hector. "I forgot. We'll look it up in the dictionary."

This is what Brenda and Hector found when they looked up the word *obelisk* in a dictionary:

> **ob e lisk** (ob′ə lisk), a tapering, four-sided shaft of stone with a top shaped like a pyramid. See picture. *noun.*
>
> From Scott, Foresman *Beginning Dictionary*.

On the page with the word *obelisk*, Brenda and Hector found a photograph in color. The picture showed them that an obelisk looks like the shape at the top of the next page.

Exercise A

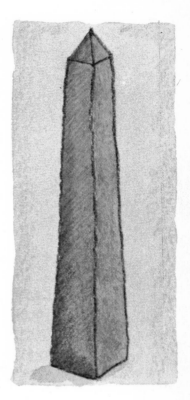

Talk about the answers to the questions below. Look at page 116 if you need help.

1. How many sides does an obelisk have?
2. What is the top of an obelisk shaped like?
3. In your own words, what is an obelisk?
4. Look up the word *obelisk* in the dictionary you use. What meaning does it give? Is there a picture of an obelisk?
5. What does the picture on pages 114–115 have to do with an obelisk?

Exercise B

Here are some other shapes whose names you may come across in your reading. Match each shape to one of the words listed below. After you match the shape and the word, check your answer by looking the word up in a dictionary.

1. tepee   2. pyramid   3. wigwam

2 Alphabetical Order

Did you have trouble looking up the words *obelisk, pyramid, tepee,* and *wigwam?* How did you know where to find these words in a dictionary? A dictionary is a list of words arranged in a certain order. How are the words arranged?

Look at the words listed below. If you know the order in which they are arranged, you know how words are arranged in a dictionary.

1. actor	3. cavity	5. enter	7. gum
2. bean	4. dream	6. film	8. house

The words in a dictionary are arranged in alphabetical order.

Exercise A

Write the numerals 1 to 12 on your paper. Then write the following words in alphabetical order.

tripod	summer	coat	quick
leopard	easy	monkey	zebra
inside	boat	alphabet	noodle

Exercise B

Write the numerals 1 to 26 on your paper. Then write, in alphabetical order, one word for each letter of the alphabet. If you can't think of a word for a letter, look in your dictionary.

Words that begin with the same letter are grouped together in a dictionary. Words that begin with the letter *a* come first. Words that begin with the letter *b* come next, and so on, from *c* to *z*. But how are words that begin with the same letter arranged?

Look at the following words. Tell which letter decides alphabetical order.

1. game   3. ghost   5. glow   7. goat
2. germ   4. girl   6. glue   8. gone

Words that begin with the same letter are arranged in alphabetical order by a letter that comes after the first letter.

Exercise C

Write the numerals 1 to 9 on your paper. Then write the following words in alphabetical order. Remember to check letters after the first letter.

meadow   million   melt
mild   mill   machine
mice   medal   milk

Exercise D

Make up sentences using only words that begin with the same letter. Here is an example: *Ants and airplanes are almost always awkward.*

119

3 Finding a Word Quickly

Suppose you are looking for the word *monsoon* in your dictionary. Where would you open your dictionary to begin looking for it? Would you open it at the front, in the middle, or at the back?

If you divide your dictionary into three equal parts, this is what you would find.

1. Words that begin with the letters *a, b, c, d,* and *e* are in the front part.
2. Words that begin with the letters *f, g, h, i, j, k, l, m, n, o,* and *p* are in the middle part.
3. Words that begin with the letters *q, r, s, t, u, v, w, x, y,* and *z* are in the back part.

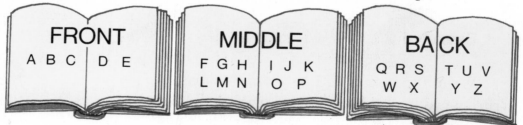

FRONT
A B C   D E

MIDDLE
F G H   I J K
L M N   O P

BACK
Q R S   T U V
W X   Y Z

 Exercise A

Write the headings *Front, Middle,* and *Back* across the top of your paper. Decide which of the following words belong under each heading. Then write the words under each heading in alphabetical order.

street	friend	jump	corn
movie	nature	willow	jeep
bump	under	yellow	school
joy	elevator	break	money

Open your dictionary somewhere in the middle and look at the top of the page. What do you see there? The two words printed in heavy black type are *guide words*. They are there to guide you to the word you are looking for. Look at these guide words from a page in a dictionary.

monitor	324	moonstone

The first guide word *monitor* tells you what word is listed first on that page. The second guide word *moonstone* tells you what word is listed last on the page. Remember that all words in a dictionary are listed in alphabetical order.

Exercise B

Tell which of the following words you would find on the page with the guide words above.

monk	monster	mop	moon
moose	money	monkey	monsoon
moo	monarch	more	month

Exercise C

Look up the words listed below in a dictionary. Then write the guide words for the page on which you find each listed word.

1. sturdy
2. angel
3. hiccup
4. porch
5. edge
6. verb
7. hundred
8. onion
9. woman

4 The Entry Word

Each word listed in a dictionary is called an *entry word.* Entry words are printed in heavy black type.

Exercise A

Look at the following part of a page from a dictionary. Then answer the questions below.

pear \'paər, 'peər\ *n* : the fleshy fruit that grows on a tree related to the apple and is commonly larger at the end opposite the stem

pearl \'pərl\ *n* **1** : a smooth body with a rich luster that is formed within the shell of some mollusks (as the **pearl oyster** of tropical seas) usually around something irritating (as a grain of sand) which has gotten into the shell **2** : MOTHER-OF-PEARL **3** : something like a pearl in shape, color, or value **4** : a pale bluish gray color

pearly \'pər-lē\ *adj* **pearl·i·er; pearl·i·est** : like a pearl especially in having a shining surface

peas·ant \'pez-nt\ *n* : a farmer owning a small amount of land or a farm worker in European countries

pease *pl of* PEA

peat \'pēt\ *n* : a blackish or dark brown material that is the remains of plants partly decayed in water and is dug and dried for use as fuel

peat moss *n* : a spongy brownish moss of wet areas that is often the chief plant making up peat

peb·ble \'peb-əl\ *n* : a small rounded stone

pe·can \pi-'kän, -'kan\ *n* : an oval edible nut that usually has a thin shell and is the fruit of a tall tree of the central and southern United States related to the walnuts

peacock

1. What are the guide words on this page?
2. How many entry words are there on this part of the page?
3. What is the first entry word on this part of the page? The fifth? The ninth?

122

A dictionary is more than just a list of words. It is also a book that gives you information about the words it lists. An entry word and the information about it are together called an *entry*.

What kind of information can you learn about a word from a dictionary? Exercise B will help you find out.

Exercise B

Look at the following entry from one dictionary. Then talk about how a dictionary can help the people described below.

chandelier A kind of light that hangs from the ceiling. Most chandeliers have several lights arranged on branches.
chan·de·lier (shand′əl ēr′) *noun, plural* **chandeliers.**

From *BEGINNING DICTIONARY*, Macmillan Publishing Co., Inc.
Copyright © 1976, 1975 Macmillan Publishing Co., Inc.
Reprinted by permission of the publisher.

1. George was writing a report about his visit to the White House. He wanted to tell about a chandelier he saw there, but he wasn't sure how to spell the word.

2. Louise was getting ready to read a story to the class. She saw the word *chandelier,* but she didn't know how to pronounce it.

3. Andy was reading a story about palaces. He saw the word *chandelier,* but he didn't know what it meant.

123

5 The Meaning of Words

There are many things you can learn about a word from a dictionary. One of the most important is the meaning of a word.

Exercise A

Look at the dictionary entries on this page to answer these questions:

1. What does an *odometer* measure?
2. What would you do with a *quoit?*
3. Where would you go to see *vaudeville?*
4. What would you find in a *cistern?*
5. What would you find in a *cruet?*
6. Where would you see a *nebula?*

---

cis·tern \'sis-tərn\ *n* : an artificial reservoir or tank for storing water usually underground

cru·et \'krü-ət\ *n* : a bottle for holding vinegar, oil, or sauce for table use

neb·u·la \'neb-yə-lə\ *n, pl* **neb·u·las** *or* **neb·u·lae** \-,lē\ : any of many clouds of gas or dust seen in the sky among the stars

odom·e·ter \ō-'däm-ət-ər\ *n* : an instrument for measuring the distance traveled (as by a vehicle)

quoit \'kwāt, 'kwȯit\ *n* : a ring (as of rope) tossed at a peg in a game (**quoits**)

vaude·ville \'vȯd-ə-vəl, 'vȯd-vəl\ *n* : theatrical entertainment made up of a variety of songs, dances, and comic acts

By permission. From *Webster's Beginning Dictionary* © 1980 by G. & C. Merriam Co., Publishers of the Merriam-Webster Dictionaries.

Many words have more than one meaning. When an entry shows more than one meaning, a numeral comes before each meaning.

Exercise B

Look at the dictionary entries on this page. Then answer these questions:

1. How many meanings does the word *nursery* have?
2. Which meaning of *nursery* would a gardener probably use?
3. How many meanings does the word *dugout* have?
4. Which meaning of *dugout* would a baseball fan probably use?

dug·out \'dəg-,aut\ *n* **1** : a boat made by hollowing out a log **2** : a shelter dug in a hillside or in the ground **3** : a low shelter facing a baseball diamond and containing the players' bench

nurs·ery \'nər-sə-rē, 'nərs-rē\ *n, pl* **nurs·er·ies** **1** : a place set aside for small children or for the care of small children **2** : a place where young trees, vines, and plants are grown and usually sold

By permission. From *Webster's Beginning Dictionary* © 1980 by G. & C. Merriam Co., Publishers of the Merriam-Webster Dictionaries.

Exercise C

Write one sentence for each of the meanings of the entry words on this page.

6 Understanding Meanings

There are several ways in which an entry can help you to understand the meaning of a word. Look at the following entry. How does it help you to understand the meaning of *hedgehog?*

** **hedgehog**   An animal that eats insects. It has a pointed snout and sharp, hard spines on its back and sides. When it is frightened or attacked, it rolls up into a ball with only its spines showing. **hedge·hog** (hej'-hog') *noun, plural* **hedgehogs.**

Hedgehog

An entry sometimes shows a picture that can help you to understand the meaning of the word.

Exercise A

Talk about five pictures in your dictionary that help you to understand the meanings of words.

Now look at the following entry. How does it help you to understand the meaning of *grime?*

** **grime**   Dirt that is covering or rubbed into a surface. The windows were covered with *grime.* **grime** (grīm) *noun.*

An entry sometimes gives you an example of how a word is used. The example helps you to understand the meaning of the word.

Exercise B

Find five entries in your dictionary that give examples of how words are used. Talk about them in class. Then find five entries that do not give examples. Write your own examples for these words.

MORE PRACTICE

A. Write the numerals 1 to 15 on your paper. Then write the following words in alphabetical order.

stone	anyone	shine	when	little
where	lard	drudge	large	zest
shiver	carpet	spoil	soap	flame

B. Write the guide words from the pages on which you find the following words in your dictionary.

1. troop   3. carousel   5. banana
2. quiet   4. jelly   6. orange

C. Look up the following words in your dictionary. Then write a sentence for each meaning of each word.

1. breathe   3. hero   5. reader
2. drumstick   4. trio   6. apron

7 Using an Index

It is easy to find a word in a dictionary because all the words are listed in alphabetical order. But many other books have information that is not arranged in alphabetical order. How do you find information in that kind of book?

Exercise A

Turn to page 317 in this book. Then answer the following questions.

1. What is this part of the book called?
2. What kind of information does the index list?
3. How are topics in the index arranged?
4. What do the numerals after each topic tell?

An index lists the topics of a book in alphabetical order. It also lists the page numbers where each topic is found.

Some topics in an index list other topics below them in alphabetical order. For example, if you can't find a page number for the body of a friendly letter under "Body," you will find it under "Friendly letters."

Exercise B

Look up the following topics in the index of this book. Write the page numbers for each one.

1. Sign language
2. Outlining
3. Index
4. Comma after closing of letter
5. Following directions

Using a Table of Contents

How can you tell what is in a book even before you read it?

Exercise A

Turn to page iii in this book. Then answer the following questions.

1. What is this part of the book called?
2. What kind of information does the table of contents, or the contents, list?
3. How are the headings in the table of contents arranged?
4. What does the numeral to the right of each heading tell?

The table of contents lists the headings in the order in which they come in the book. The number to the right of each heading shows the page on which the heading appears. The table of contents always comes at the beginning of a book.

Exercise B

Write the numerals 1 to 10 on your paper. Then turn to the table of contents in this book. Write the headings you will find on the following pages. Which headings give the name of a unit? Which headings give the name of a lesson?

1. 10   3. 32   5. 74   7. 92   9. 145
2. 31   4. 48   6. 76   8. 120   10. 177

9 Using Your Language

In earlier units, you chose between two ways to say or write something. The box below shows some of the choices you made. If you need more help with the exercise, turn to the table of contents. It will help you find the "Using Your Language" lessons for Units One, Two, Three, and Four.

SAY AND WRITE . . .	NOT . . .
1. She ate an apple.	1. She ate a apple.
2. Dan and I whistled.	2. Me and Dan whistled.
3. He saw June and me.	3. He saw me and June.
4. He doesn't have any fun.	4. He doesn't have no fun.
or	
He has no fun.	
5. I read those books.	5. I read them books.

Exercise

Write each sentence. Choose a word at the left for the box.

(a, an)   1. We saw ☐ owl in ☐ tree.
(a, an)   2. ☐ old bus hit ☐ new car.
(any, no)   3. He couldn't eat ☐ sugar.
(any, no)   4. Susan hasn't ☐ toys to play with.
(them, those)   5. Do you like ☐ shoes?
(Them, Those)   6. ☐ snakes are not asleep.

Review

Write the following story. Change sentences to make them better. Remember the following hints as you write the story.

1. When you name someone else with yourself, name yourself last.
2. Use *a* before a word that begins with a consonant sound. Use *an* before a word that begins with a vowel sound.
3. Do not use *no* and *not* in the same sentence when only one of them is needed.
4. Never use *them* to signal a noun.

"Why are you carrying them suitcases?" asked Troy. "Where are you going?"

"Me and Harry are going on a airplane to visit our cousins in Hobart," said Sylvia. "I don't have no time to talk to you now. I have to catch a early bus for the airport."

"I wish I could fly on an plane," said Troy, "but I don't have no cousins I can visit."

"Maybe you can come and visit me and Harry next week," said Sylvia. "I'll write you a note when I get there."

"Send me one of them funny picture postcards," said Troy. "Me and my brother like to collect all kinds. We don't have no postcards from Hobart."

"OK," said Sylvia. "I hope you'll be able to visit Harry and me. Good-bye."

EDITING EXERCISE

In this unit, you learned about words in a dictionary. You know that dictionary words are listed in ABC order. You also know that words can be used and grouped in many different ways. Words can tell a story or a joke. They can give directions or ask a riddle. In the poems that follow, you will see how poets choose their words with special care. Along the way, you will have some fun with a parrot, an elephant, and a squirrel or two.

THE PARROT

The parrot is
    A *talking* bird.
He says real words
    That he has heard.

And he repeats
    His words, although
Just what they mean
    He doesn't know!

ILO ORLEANS

STRETCHING

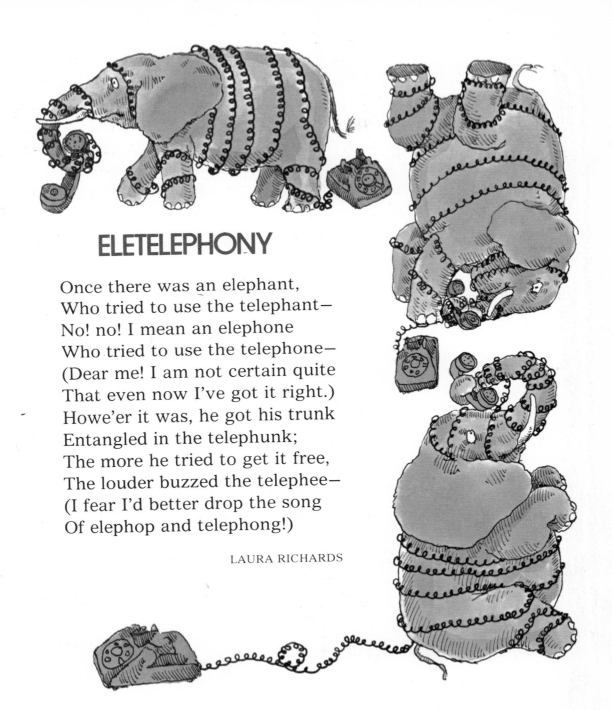

ELETELEPHONY

Once there was an elephant,
Who tried to use the telephant—
No! no! I mean an elephone
Who tried to use the telephone—
(Dear me! I am not certain quite
That even now I've got it right.)
Howe'er it was, he got his trunk
Entangled in the telephunk;
The more he tried to get it free,
The louder buzzed the telephee—
(I fear I'd better drop the song
Of elephop and telephong!)

LAURA RICHARDS

YOUR IMAGINATION

BRISKY FRISKY

Brisky Frisky,
Hipperty hop,
Up he goes
To the tree top!

Whirly, twirly,
Round and round,
Down he scampers
To the ground.

Furly, curly,
What a tail.
Tall as a feather,
Broad as a snail.

Where's his supper?
In the shell.
Snappy, cracky,
Out it fell.

ANONYMOUS

The Question Mark

The squirrel is a-hurrying
    And scurrying around;
He's looking for a nut that he
    Once buried in the ground.

His tail is like a question mark.
    The question on his mind
Is, why his buried treasure
    Is hard for him to find.

ILO ORLEANS

Now it's your turn to use words in special ways. Get ready to s-t-r-e-t-c-h your imagination.

Exercise A

In the poem "Eletelephony," the writer kept getting parts of words mixed up. For example, she mixed *telephone* and *elephant* and came up with *telephant*. Make five mixed-up words of your own. Ask the class to figure out the two words you mixed up.

Exercise B

Not all the words in "Brisky Frisky" are real words. Talk about what you think the poet means by *brisky*, *furly*, and *cracky*. What does a squirrel do when it goes "hipperty hop"?

Exercise C

Does a squirrel's tail look like a question mark? Some words can be made to look like what they mean. Look at the word pictures below. Then make three word pictures of your own.

Reviewing Your Skills

The page numerals after each heading show you where to look if you need help with this review.

Using Alphabetical Order (118–119)

Write the numerals 1 to 12 on your paper. Then write the following words in alphabetical order.

solid	trunk	milk
ant	orange	boot
yellow	crate	free
fight	lesson	worry

Using Guide Words (121)

Tell which of the following words you would find on a dictionary page with the guide words **battle** and **bright**.

beautiful	buy	burst	break
awful	bought	block	bread
believe	blank	bold	boundary
big	carry	bad	bar

Finding the Meanings of Words (124–127)

Look up the following words in your dictionary. Then write a sentence for each meaning of each word.

1. letter
2. school
3. dish
4. prize
5. thread
6. bread

Using an Index (128)

Look up the following topics in the index of this book. Write the pages for each topic.

1. Note taking
2. Guide words in dictionary
3. Poetry
4. ZIP (Zoning Improvement Plan) code
5. Quotation marks
6. Plural forms

Using Your Language (24–25, 44–45, 76–77, 102–103, 130–131)

Write each sentence. Choose a word or words at the left for the box.

(a, an)   **1.** I heard ☐ owl hoot.

(a, an)   **2.** We had ☐ early dinner last night.

(any, no)   **3.** Jackie didn't swim in ☐ races.

(any, no)   **4.** Some cats haven't ☐ tails.

(I and Lee, Lee and I)   **5.** ☐ set up the hurdles.

(Dad and I, I and Dad)   **6.** ☐ waxed the skis.

(Them, Those)   **7.** ☐ lizards can grow new tails.

(them, those)   **8.** Let me help you deliver ☐ papers.

(a, an)   **9.** I have ☐ idea for ☐ skit.

(any, none)   **10.** I haven't seen ☐ of my friends today.

(Them, Those)   **11.** ☐ plants have poisonous leaves.

(a, an)   **12.** We waited half ☐ hour for ☐ bus.

Testing Your Skills

Using Alphabetical Order

Write the numerals 1 to 15 on your paper. Then write the following words in alphabetical order.

battle	mud	worm
year	wheel	army
cucumber	early	defense
hotel	niece	inch
got	jumble	field

Using Guide Words

Tell which of the following words you would find on a dictionary page with the guide words **pat** and **phase.**

pass	pattern	patch	pea
peach	post	press	pot
pave	paw	pebble	plunge
pole	patrol	pipe	peace
preach	pull	peel	pen

Finding the Meanings of Words

Look up the following words in your dictionary. Then write a sentence for each meaning of each word.

1. cold   **3.** handle   **5.** fish

2. engineer   **4.** rose   **6.** jungle

Using an Index

Look up the following topics in the index of this book. Write the pages for each topic.

1. Explaining paragraphs
2. Addresses on envelope
3. Reading aloud
4. Naming yourself last
5. Predicate of sentences
6. Singular and plural forms

Using Your Language

Write each sentence. Choose a word or words at the left for the box.

(a, an)　　　　　**1.** Add ☐ onion to the stew.

(A, An)　　　　　**2.** ☐ angry customer wanted a refund.

(any, no)　　　　**3.** I don't see ☐ cucumbers on the vines.

(any, no)　　　　**4.** You haven't ☐ sense of humor.

(I and Ted, Ted and I)　**5.** ☐ traded lunches.

(Them, Those)　　**6.** ☐ sandwiches tasted good.

(a, an)　　　　　**7.** There's ☐ insect on your back.

(any, no)　　　　**8.** Don't you like ☐ vegetables?

(them, those)　　**9.** Who built ☐ kites?

(any, no)　　　　**10.** This kite hasn't ☐ string.

(I and Pat, Pat and I)　**11.** ☐ solved the problem.

(a, an)　　　　　**12.** ☐ octopus grabbed ☐ eel.

(Them, Those)　　**13.** ☐ packages look heavy.

(a, an)　　　　　**14.** Help yourself to ☐ ear of corn.

(any, no)　　　　**15.** There isn't ☐ icing on the cake.

Skills Checkup

Putting Words in Order (10–11)

Change the order of the words in each group below to make a sentence.

1. the made mayor an announcement
2. the slid off the table tray
3. parents my have gone work to
4. our a child adopted neighbors have
5. dinner oven is in the

Finding Key Words (14–15)

Write each sentence. Draw a line under the key word in the subject. Draw two lines under the key word in the predicate.

1. A deer leaped over the fence.
2. The beans cooked for hours.
3. The phone rang once.
4. The children sold lemonade.
5. The boy chased a firefly.

Writing Statements and Questions (17–18)

A. Write each group of words below as a statement:

1. the horse is eating oats
2. this is your book
3. you are finished with your story
4. that bird is a robin
5. the bus will leave soon

B. Write each group of words in Part A as a question.

Putting Events in Order (38)

Put the events below in order:

1. Scouts go camping
2. Scouts cook fish
3. Scouts look for firewood
4. Then, scouts go fishing
5. First, scouts set up tents

Writing Titles (41)

Write each title. Use capital letters where they are
needed.

1. a day at the shore
2. time to travel
3. the first day of school
4. the happiest boy in town
5. pets in our house

6. the blue balloon
7. a ride in the country
8. our new house
9. a fishing trip
10. strange animals at the zoo

Showing That Someone Is Speaking (42–43)

Write the sentences below. Use commas, capital letters,
and quotation marks to show that someone is speaking.

1. pam said it is easy to row a boat
2. her father said you must be careful
3. rick warned don't stand up in the boat
4. pam complained my arms are getting tired
5. rick offered let me help you row

Skills
Checkup

Finding Nouns in the Subject and the Predicate (58–59)

Write each sentence below. Draw a slash mark between the subject and the predicate. Then circle each noun you find in the subject and the predicate.

1. The scouts gathered firewood.
2. The kite had a long tail.
3. A car blocked the driveway.
4. The eagle spotted a mouse.
5. The actor held the script.
6. The athlete ran a fast race.

Writing Plural Nouns (62–63)

Write the plural form of each of the following singular nouns:

1. bench
2. peach
3. flash
4. bus
5. miss
6. gas
7. breeze
8. box

Writing Possessive Nouns (64–65)

Write each sentence below. Use the possessive form of the noun at the left for the box in each sentence.

(catcher)   1. A ☐ mask was lying near the bench.

(neighbor)   2. Ned mows our ☐ lawn.

(doctor)   3. Obey the ☐ orders.

(bird)   4. A ☐ feather decorated the hat.

(rooster)   5. The ☐ crow woke me.

(players)   6. I collect baseball ☐ autographs.

142

Writing a Friendly Letter (88–96)

Put the five parts of the friendly letter in order. Write them correctly as parts of the same letter.

1. your best friend
2. 13 yardly road
   marietta georgia 30060
   june 15 19--
3. eileen
4. dear lisa
5. i'm enclosing a picture of my new home isn't it pretty i miss you very much i hope you will write to me soon tell everyone in school i miss them

Addressing Envelopes (96)

Ms. Carroll is sending a letter to Ms. Damien. Draw an envelope. Fill in the return address and the address.

ms lottie carroll   ms martha damien
p o box 668   3123 school street
essex connecticut 06426   columbia south carolina 29202

Sending Postcards (101)

Cut out a 6-inch by 9-inch piece of paper. Draw or paste a picture on one side. Draw a line down the center of the other side. Write a note on the left side. Address it on the right side.

Learning About Verbs

GRAMMAR	How Verbs Show Time Verbs That Add *-ed* Verbs That Do Not Add *-ed* Words That Help Verbs
COMPOSITION	Making Sentences Grow
MECHANICS	Contractions
VOCABULARY	Sound Words Words That Speak and Move
USAGE	Using *run* or *ran; come* or *came; is* or *are; was* or *were*

In Unit Three, you explored what nouns and pronouns do in the sentence. In this unit, you will look at verbs and at what they do in the sentence.

145

1 What Do Verbs Do?

Different kinds of words do different things in a sentence. Some words name persons, places, or things. What do you call these words?

Nouns name persons, places, and things.

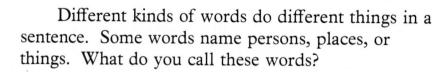

Exercise A

Use nouns to name the persons, places, and things that you see in the picture on pages 144–145. Write a list of the nouns you used. Then read your list to the class. Did everybody use the same nouns to name the persons, places, and things they saw? Talk about the different nouns. Talk about pronouns that can substitute for nouns.

Nouns and pronouns are important in sentences, but they need help from another kind of word. What kind of word has been left out of each sentence in this story?

The acrobat ☐ the swinging bar. She ☐ through the air to the other side of the circus tent. Then she ☐ her hold on the bar. The crowd ☐. The acrobat ☐ into the net. She ☐ quickly to her feet. Then she ☐ to the crowd.

Read the story again. This time pay special attention to the verbs that have been added. What do the verbs do?

The acrobat grabbed the swinging bar. She flew through the air to the other side of the circus tent. Then she lost her hold on the bar. The crowd gasped. The acrobat fell into the net. She jumped quickly to her feet. Then she waved to the crowd.

A verb usually tells what a person or thing does or is.

Exercise B

Look at the list of nouns that you wrote in Exercise A. Use each noun as the subject of a sentence. Then write a verb that tells what that person or thing does.

Exercise C

Use each verb in the story on this page in a sentence of your own.

147

2 Verbs in Sentences

Read this sentence:

The squirrel / climbed the tree.

Find the subject of the sentence. Find the predicate. Which word in the predicate tells what the squirrel did? Does the verb *climbed* come after the subject?

The verb in a sentence usually comes after the subject.

 Exercise A

Write each sentence. Put a slash mark between the subject and the predicate. Draw a line under the verb.

1. Ducks splashed in the pond.
2. Orville flew an airplane.
3. The runner fell down.
4. Amy caught the ball.
5. Trees shaded the park.
6. My cat chased me.
7. The woman rode the horse.
8. Cows eat grass.
9. Paco caught a fish.
10. Athletes run races.
11. Tex found a dollar.
12. Rangers save trees.

Exercise B

Think about verbs that will fit in the boxes in the following sentences. See how many different verbs you can think of for each box. Then write the sentences using one of the verbs in each box.

1. Jerry ☐ the cake.
2. The car ☐ down the hill.
3. Maria ☐ a birdhouse.
4. Nobody ☐ the movie.
5. My aunt ☐ her car.
6. I ☐ an old book.
7. The flowers ☐.
8. Mr. Benson ☐ an orange.
9. Andy ☐ the actor.
10. She ☐ the horse.
11. The rocket ☐ through space.
12. The bear ☐ a fish.
13. We ☐ a squirrel.
14. The magician ☐ the trick.
15. The fish ☐ in the water.

Facts About Language

The sentence in which a word is used can be a meaning clue: (a) I drank two *glasses* of lemonade. (2) He broke his reading *glasses*.

Exercise C

Draw a slash mark between the subject and predicate of each sentence you wrote for Exercise B.

149

3 How Some Verbs Show Time

Look at the underlined verbs in the following sentences.

1. My sisters <u>collect</u> baseball cards.
2. My brother <u>collects</u> bugs.

Do the verbs in these two sentences tell about something that is happening now? The verb forms *collect* and *collects* show present time.

Now look at the underlined verb in this sentence:

We <u>collected</u> two pounds of paper.

Does the verb in this sentence tell about something that has already happened? The verb *collected* shows past time. With what two letters does *collected* end?

Most verbs that show past time end in -ed.

Exercise A

Write the past form of each verb. When *-ed* is added to a verb that ends in *e*, what happens to the first *e?*

1. sign
2. save
3. turn
4. walk
5. wave
6. wash
7. help
8. skate

150

Exercise B

Write each sentence. Draw a line under the verb. Tell whether the verb shows present time or past time.

1. We skated across the lake.
2. Wendell works on Saturdays.
3. She banged the drum slowly.
4. I waited an hour to get in.
5. The comet whirled through space.
6. Mom turned off the TV.

Exercise C

Use each verb below in two sentences. In the first sentence, show present time. In the second sentence, show past time.

1. miss   2. start   3. love   4. jump   5. help

Exercise D

The sentences below show present time. Write the sentences to show past time.

1. He picks flowers in the park.
2. Cory shoves into line.
3. Maryann closes the trunk.
4. Andrew mends his clothes.
5. We start a new club today.
6. The rain washes the streets.

151

More About Verbs and Time

Look at the underlined verbs in the following sentences.

1. Rabbits <u>run</u> fast.
2. I <u>ran</u> twice around the block.

Which verb shows present time? Which verb shows past time? Does *ran* end in *-ed?*

Some verbs have special forms to show past time.

Here are some of the verbs that have special forms to show past time:

PRESENT		PAST
come	comes	came
do	does	did
drive	drives	drove
eat	eats	ate
give	gives	gave
go	goes	went
grow	grows	grew
know	knows	knew
make	makes	made
run	runs	ran
see	sees	saw
sing	sings	sang
take	takes	took
write	writes	wrote

Exercise

Read each sentence. Tell whether the verb shows present time or past time.

1. He sang the National Anthem.
2. Birds eat bread crumbs.
3. My cousins came by train.
4. They know the conductor.
5. The family went to Boston.
6. Sarah made a bowl of punch.
7. It took two hours to get there.
8. We drove through a tunnel.
9. The town gave her a parade.
10. That hat goes with those gloves.

MORE PRACTICE

Write each sentence. Underline the verb in each one and tell whether it shows present or past time.

1. Kangaroos jump a lot.
2. I wrote a story about a lizard.
3. A spider touched my arm.
4. The waves make lots of noise.
5. Jim's uncle drove the wagon.
6. We saw a great movie.
7. Jenny planted a rosebush.
8. She does it every year.
9. Cinderella scrubbed the floor.
10. I believe you.

153

5 Words That Help Verbs

The words *have, has,* and *had* sometimes help verbs to show time. Read these sentences:

1. She <u>walked</u> across the grass.
2. We <u>have walked</u> for two days.

With what two letters does the verb in sentence 1 end? Find the helping word in sentence 2. With what two letters does the verb it helps end?

> **The helping words *have, has,* and *had* are sometimes used with a form of the verb that ends in *-ed.***

Now read these sentences:

1. She <u>wrote</u> a short story.
2. He <u>has written</u> a long poem.

In sentence 1, the verb *wrote* is the past form of *write.* Find the helping word in sentence 2. What verb does it help? Does the verb end in *-ed?*

> **Some verbs have a special form that is used with the helping words *have, has,* and *had.***

See the top of the next page for some of the verbs with special forms that are used with *have, has,* and *had:*

154

PRESENT		PAST	HAVE/HAS/HAD
come	comes	came	come
do	does	did	done
drive	drives	drove	driven
eat	eats	ate	eaten
go	goes	went	gone
grow	grows	grew	grown
know	knows	knew	known
run	runs	ran	run
see	sees	saw	seen
take	takes	took	taken

Exercise A

Write each sentence. Draw a line under the verb. Circle the helping word.

1. I had seen that movie already.
2. She has taken her last test.
3. The geese have gone south.
4. You have eaten my cookie.
5. The baby has grown an inch.

Exercise B

Write your own sentences. Use a helping word with the special form of each verb below. Use the chart above if you need help.

1. take	**3.** know	**5.** go	**7.** see
2. come	**4.** do	**6.** eat	**8.** drive

155

6 More About Helping Words

The words *am, is, are, was,* and *were* are used as helping words. Read these sentences:

1. I sing slow songs only.
2. I am singing a lullaby now.

Find the helping word in sentence 2. With what three letters does the verb it helps end?

The helping words *am, is, are, was,* and *were* are used with a form of the verb that ends in *-ing*.

Exercise A

Write the following sentences. Draw a line under the verb. Circle the helping word.

1. The crowd was screaming.
2. My shoes are hurting me.
3. Sandra is smiling at you.
4. The boys were humming a song.
5. I am running downtown.
6. The dry leaves are falling.
7. The sun is shining brightly.
8. I am keeping score for our team.
9. Lester was sleeping in the car.
10. Mom and I were counting stars.

Write the sentences below. Circle each helping word and draw a line under the verb it helps.

1. Jan was running, and we were screaming.
2. We were playing the game "Red Rover."
3. Our team has won, and the others have gone.
4. Mom had played "Red Rover" years ago.

MORE PRACTICE

A. Write the following sentences. Use the correct word at the left for the box.

(seeing, seen)   **1.** She has ☐ him before.
(taking, taken)   **2.** I was ☐ a walk.
(stopping, stopped)   **3.** The train is ☐ here.
(winning, won)   **4.** Our team has ☐ a game.
(rubbing, rubbed)   **5.** Billy is ☐ his head.
(looking, looked)   **6.** Carol was ☐ for you.

B. Write the following sentences. Use the correct helping word for the box in each one.

(are, have)   **1.** The bells ☐ ringing.
(is, has)   **2.** Kelly ☐ sunning herself.
(is, has)   **3.** It ☐ taken me two years.
(are, have)   **4.** They ☐ playing checkers.
(am, have)   **5.** I ☐ driven a jeep.

7 Contractions

Look at the following sentences:

1. <u>I am</u> going out.
2. <u>I'm</u> going out.

What two words make up the underlined word in sentence 2? What mark is used to show that a letter is missing? The underlined word in sentence 2 is a contraction.

A contraction is made up of two words written together with one or more letters left out. An apostrophe takes the place of the missing letter or letters.

Some contractions are made up of pronouns and helping words:

I	+ am going	= I'm going
we	+ are going	= we're going
he	+ is going	= he's going
they	+ have gone	= they've gone

Exercise A

Write these pronouns and helping words as contractions:

1. they are   **3.** it is   **5.** she is

2. you are   **4.** you have   **6.** we have

Exercise B

Write the following sentences. Draw a line under each contraction. Tell what two words make up the contraction.

1. She's driving to Mexico.
2. They're getting a new coach.
3. I've never seen that one before.
4. We're going on a picnic.
5. It's raining in California.
6. You've taken the wrong turn.
7. I'm leaving soon.
8. They've stopped shouting.

Some contractions are made up of a helping word and *not:*

are, is, was	+ not = aren't, isn't, wasn't
were, have, has	+ not = weren't, haven't, hasn't
had	+ not = hadn't

Exercise C

Write the following sentences. Change the underlined words in each sentence into a contraction.

1. I have not told anyone.
2. She is looking for you.
3. You are not fooling me.
4. You are not fooling me.
5. That was not what I said.

Making Sentences Grow

In Unit One, you learned that a sentence is made up of two parts. What are the two parts of a sentence?

In Unit Three, you learned how to make a sentence grow by adding words that tell about, or describe, a noun in the subject or predicate.

Read these sentences:

1. George / ran.
2. George / ran quickly down the street.

Have the new words in sentence 2 been added to the subject or the predicate? Do *quickly* and *down the street* tell about a verb or a noun? You can make a sentence grow by adding words that tell about, or describe, the verb.

Words that describe the verb can tell *how,* *where,* or *when.* Look at this sentence:

The stars shine <u>brightly</u> <u>in the sky</u> <u>at night.</u>

Which word tells how the stars shine? Which words tell where the stars shine? Which words tell when the stars shine?

Now watch another sentence grow:

1. Gulls fly.
2. Gulls fly slowly.
3. Gulls fly slowly and gracefully.
4. Gulls fly slowly and gracefully across the sky.

Write the sentences below. Make each one grow by adding words that describe the verb.

1. The plane flew.
2. Jane danced.
3. Most people work.
4. The frogs splashed.
5. **The children played.**
6. The water roared.
7. Monkeys swing.
8. All of us laughed.
9. The cold wind blew.
10. The ladder fell.

The person who wrote about a birthday surprise used dull verbs. Edit the story. Use lively verbs. Make each sentence grow by adding words to the subject and the predicate. Make other changes that are needed.

the birthday surprise
lee got out of bed she went into the kitchen a package moved the package came open a puppy went to lee

EDITING EXERCISE

9 Working with Words

Where do words come from? Many people believe that words are named after sounds. For example, what sound do the brakes make when a car comes to a sudden stop?

The brakes screeched.

The verb *screeched* sounds like the sound made by the brakes.

Exercise A

What kind of sound do the words at the left make you think of? Read each sentence at the right. Then decide which word belongs in which box.

Sound Words

hummed   **1.** The rain ☐ against the window.

clicked   **2.** My heels ☐ along the hall.

tapped   **3.** The children ☐ with the music.

roared   **4.** Mom's key ☐ in the lock.

spattered   **5.** The lion ☐ at its trainer.

Here are two more sound words:

whisper YELL

Exercise B

Think of other verbs for different kinds of speaking. Draw a picture to go with one of the verbs you think of.

162

Now read this poem:

Cats purr.   Monkeys chatter.
Lions roar.   Cows moo.
Owls hoot.   Ducks quack.
Bears snore.   Doves coo.
Crickets creak.   Pigs squeal.
Mice squeak.   Horses neigh.
Sheep baa.   Chickens cluck.
But I SPEAK!   But I SAY!

Flies hum.
Dogs growl.
Bats screech.
Coyotes howl.
Frogs croak.
Parrots squawk.
Bees buzz
But I TALK!

ARNOLD L. SHAPIRO

**Words
That Speak
and Move**

![pencil] **Exercise C**

Think of a verb that tells how each animal
named below moves. Write the noun and the verb
in a sentence.

1. Worms   3. Rabbits   5. Horses
2. Snakes   4. Birds   6. Ducks

10 Using Your Language

Look at the verbs in the following sentences:

1. I <u>run</u> every day.
2. He <u>ran</u> a good race.
3. He <u>has</u> <u>run</u> two miles today.

The verb in sentence 1 shows present time. What time does the verb in sentence 2 show? In which sentence does the verb have a helping word?

The word *ran* is always used by itself to show past time. The word *run* is used by itself to show present time. The word *run* is also used with a helping word.

run come
or or
ran? came?

Talk about the verbs in the following sentences:

1. We <u>come</u> here every day.
2. She <u>came</u> home late.
3. They <u>have</u> <u>come</u> all the way from Toledo.

The word *came* is always used by itself to show past time. The word *come* is used by itself to show present time. *Come* is also used with a helping word.

Use the correct word at the left for the box.

(come, came)   **1.** We have ☐ to help you.
(run, ran)   **2.** She ☐ to catch the bus.
(come, came)   **3.** Ambrose ☐ in a hurry.
(run, ran)   **4.** You have ☐ enough today.
(come, came)   **5.** Elisa ☐ to my party.

Look at the underlined helping words in the following sentences.

1. This egg is turning bad.
2. Your eggs are getting cold.
3. She was working hard.
4. They were taking it easy.

Which helping words are used with singular subjects? Which helping words are used with plural subjects?

The words *is* and *was* are used with singular subjects. The words *are* and *were* are used with plural subjects.

is	was
or	or
are?	were?

Exercise B

Use the correct word at the left for the box.

(was, were)   **1.** Ray ☐ reading out loud.
(is, are)   **2.** The geese ☐ flying.
(was, were)   **3.** The logs ☐ burning.
(is, are)   **4.** This ☐ going to be fun.
(is, are)   **5.** The sun ☐ coming up.

Reviewing
Your Skills

The page numerals after each heading show you where to look if you need help with this review.

Recognizing Verbs (148–149)

Write each sentence. Draw a slash mark between the subject and the predicate. Draw a line under the verb.

1. Mark saw that movie.
2. My sister helped me.
3. Ralph likes this cereal.
4. Gina writes poetry.
5. The castle has a tower.
6. My dog sleeps outside.

Making Verbs Show Time (150–151)

Use each verb below in two sentences. In the first sentence, show present time. In the second sentence, show past time.

1. call
2. talk
3. chase
4. wash
5. paint
6. skate

Finding Verbs and Words That Help Verbs (154–157)

Write each sentence. Draw a line under the verb. Circle the helping word.

1. Joe is baking a cake.
2. The pupils are listening to a tape.
3. Toby has saved ten dollars.
4. Teresa is helping her sister.
5. My parents are driving us.
6. Your friend is calling you.

Writing Contractions (158–159)

Write the following sentences. Draw a line under each contraction. Tell what two words make up the contraction.

1. He's riding my bike.

2. They're going to the library.

3. I've lost my pen.

4. We're looking for our cat.

5. You've dialed the wrong number.

6. I'm collecting old newspapers.

Making Sentences Grow (160–161)

Write the sentences below. Make each one grow by adding words that describe the verb.

1. Children sing.

2. Monkeys play.

3. The wind blows.

4. Puppies bark.

5. Birds fly.

Using Sound Words (162–163)

What kind of sound do the words at the left make you think of? Read each sentence at the right. Then decide which word belongs in which box.

croaked   **1.** Coyotes ☐ at the moon.

squawked   **2.** The iron gates ☐ shut.

creaked   **3.** The old wooden stairs ☐ .

clanged   **4.** The frogs ☐ noisily.

howled   **5.** The parrot ☐ for food.

Testing
Your Skills

Recognizing Verbs

Write each sentence. Draw a slash mark between the subject and the predicate. Draw a line under the verb.

1. Many people watched the parade.
2. Elephants pulled the circus wagons.
3. Children rode the ponies.
4. A donkey kicked its heels.
5. A clown walked on stilts.
6. A lion growled.

Making Verbs Show Time

Use each verb below in two sentences. In the first sentence, show present time. In the second sentence, show past time.

1. wish   3. help   5. save
2. bake   4. work   6. clean

Finding Verbs and Words That Help Verbs

Write each sentence. Draw a line under the verb. Circle the helping word.

1. I am rocking the baby.
2. The baby is smiling at me.
3. Scott is playing the piano.
4. The bus is leaving now.
5. The corn is growing tall.
6. I am learning Spanish.

Writing Contractions

Write the following sentences. Draw a line under each contraction. Tell what two words make up the contraction.

1. The dogs wouldn't stop barking.
2. I'm practicing my speech.
3. The telephone isn't working.
4. He's my only cousin.
5. You're sitting in my seat.
6. They're fixing breakfast.

Making Sentences Grow

Write the sentences below. Make each one grow by adding words that describe the verb.

1. Cattle grazed.
2. A mouse ran.
3. Shoppers rushed.
4. The fans cheered.
5. The water splashed.

Using Sound Words

What kind of sound do the words at the left make you think of? Read each sentence at the right. Then decide which word belongs in which box.

rang   1. The snake ☐ at us.
buzzed   2. The doorbell ☐.
hissed   3. The train ☐ to a halt.
screeched   4. A fly ☐ near my ear.
squished   5. My wet shoes ☐ as I walked.

Skills Checkup

Finding Key Words (14–15)

Write each sentence. Draw a line under the key word in the subject. Draw two lines under the key word in the predicate.

1. The camera takes good pictures.
2. The pupils finished the project.
3. The girl caught a trout.
4. The squirrel found a peanut.
5. A chameleon changes color.

Showing That Someone Is Speaking (42–43)

Write the sentences below. Use commas, capital letters, and quotation marks to show that someone is speaking.

1. anne said i can't see the board
2. ms. darby asked where are your glasses
3. anne replied i left them at home
4. ms. darby said take a seat in the front row

Finding Nouns in the Subject and the Predicate (58–59)

Write each sentence below. Draw a slash mark between the subject and the predicate. Then circle each noun you find in the subject and the predicate.

1. The chickens ate the corn.
2. The jacket has two pockets.
3. The kitchen faces the yard.
4. The teacher speaks two languages.

Writing Plural Nouns (62–63)

Write the plural form of each of the following singular nouns:

1. page
2. class
3. pitch
4. hiss
5. girl

6. speech
7. ditch
8. dime
9. wish
10. eye

Writing a Friendly Letter (88–96)

Put the five parts of the friendly letter in order. Write them correctly as parts of the same letter.

1. your friend
2. 4790 southeast 8 street
   ocala florida 32670
   may 6 19--
3. maria
4. dear cathy
5. our class visited Planet Ocean this week my parents said that if you come to visit me this summer, they'll take us there then we can enjoy Planet Ocean together i hope that you can visit us

Using Alphabetical Order (118–119)

Write the numerals 1 to 10 on your paper. Then write the following words in alphabetical order.

beach	arrow	youth	author	creek
mirror	hammer	wander	grouch	lucky

Putting On a Play

COMPOSITION   Thinking of a Story for a
                  Play
                  Describing the
                  Characters
                  Writing the Words of a
                  Play
                  Describing the Costumes
                  and Props

SPEAKING   Showing Feelings with
                  the Voice
                  Acting Out a Play

USAGE   Using *drive* or *driven;*
                  wrote or *written; did* or
                  done

In this unit, you will act out a play. But before you do, you will explore how plays are put together. Then you will help write a play for a talking fish.

What Is a Play?

Have you ever seen a play? Perhaps you saw one in a theater with your parents. Or maybe you saw one at school. Many of the shows you see on TV are plays. And movies are really plays on film.

But what exactly is a play? A play is a story acted out by people.

When you read a story in a book, the words printed on the page tell you who the characters are, where the story takes place, and what happens in the story. But when you go to a play, you see the characters move and speak. You see *where* everything happens. You see *what* happens.

 Exercise A

Think about a play you saw in a theater, at school, on TV, or at the movies. Then write about what you saw.

1. Tell who the characters were and what they looked like.
2. Describe the place where the play occurred.
3. Then tell what happened in the story of the play.
4. Finally, tell whether you liked the play or not and why.

It takes many people to put on a play. A writer writes the play. The actors play the characters. Some people make the sets that tell you where the play takes place. Others make the costumes that the actors wear.

Exercise B

Look at the people in the picture on this page and the photograph on pages 172–173. Talk about how each one helps to make a play.

2 The Story of a Play

What is the first thing you need to make a play? The first thing you need is of course a good story.

Exercise A

Choose one of your favorite stories and think about it. Then ask the following questions about the story and talk about your answers in class.

1. Which character has a problem to solve in the story?
2. What is the problem?
3. How does the character solve the problem?

A play is like a story in three important ways. First, the beginning of the play should be interesting to the audience. Second, the events in the play should be in the right order. And third, the end of the play should help the audience remember the play. The end could be a surprise or a joke, but it should solve the problem of the play.

Exercise B

Think of a story that you want to make into a play. It can be one you read, or you can make up your own. Then write a few sentences that tell what happens in the play. Use the questions in Exercise A to help you.

The Characters in a Play 3

What do you call a person in the story of a play? A person in the story of a play, like a person in a story, is one of the characters. The story of the play tells what the characters do and say. In most plays there are usually two main characters. These main characters are the ones who have to solve the problem. And they are the ones who usually do solve it.

Exercise A

Look at the sentences you wrote in Exercise B on page 176. Then write a list of the characters that will be in your play. Put the main characters at the top of the list.

When you act in a play, you have to know the character you are playing. When you write a play, you have to know all the characters.

Facts About Language

As language grows, words take on new meanings. A *book* can be the words of a play. It can be a small bundle: a *book* of matches.

Exercise B

Look at the list of characters you wrote for Exercise A above. Write a sentence or two that describes what kind of person each character is. Your descriptions will help the actors know how to play the characters.

The Words of a Play

The characters in a play do things and say things. The story of a play tells what the characters do and say. The actors who play the characters have to know what each character says and does.

Exercise A

Look at the descriptions of the characters you wrote in Exercise B on page 177. Think about what each character does in the story of the play. Then talk about what each character would say in the play.

When you read a story, how do you know the exact words each character says? The exact words that a character in a story speaks have quotation marks around them. Usually there is a word like *said* or *asked* to introduce the exact words.

Exercise B

Read the following sentences. Then tell the exact words each person said.

1. Don said, "I think this is the key to the secret room."
2. Ann Marie whispered, "Well, let's go and find out what's in there."
3. Then Judy asked, "But what if someone catches us?"

Now read the following part of a play. Tell the exact words each character says.

> DON: I think this is the key to the secret room.
> ANN MARIE: Well, let's go and find out what's in there.
> JUDY: But what if someone catches us?

When you write the words of a play, follow these guidelines:

1. Write the character's name in capital letters.

2. Then write the exact words the character says.

3. Do not use words like *said* or *asked* to introduce the exact words.

4. Do not use quotation marks, but punctuate each sentence correctly.

Exercise C

Write the following story in the form of a play:

Bert asked, "What's that in the sky?"
Sue looked up and answered, "I think it's a flying saucer."
Bert said, "Let's get out of here fast!"

Exercise D

Think about the play you are writing and the characters in it. Then write the words that each character will say in the play.

Using Your Voice to Show Feelings

5

Have you ever read a story out loud to a group of people? Acting in a play is something like reading out loud. You have to speak loudly and clearly so that everyone can hear you. You have to say the words with meaning so that everyone understands what you are feeling. Look at the following sentence.

What a day this has been!

How would you say this sentence if you were tired? How would you say it if you were happy? How would you say it if everything had gone wrong?

Exercise A

Say each statement or question in different ways to show different feelings. The clues will help you.

1. I'm leaving. (Are you happy, sad, angry, or excited?)
2. Did Jack make this cake? (Do you like Jack? Do you like the cake?)
3. I think it's going to rain. (Do you want it to rain or not? Are you sure it will rain? Do you like rain?)

Exercise B

Read the words that you wrote for your own play out loud. Make sure you say the words with meaning.

Using Your Body

When you act in a play, you use your voice to show how a character feels. You can also show a lot about a character by the way you walk, sit, and move your body.

Exercise A

Pretend that you are each of the following characters in a play. Show how you would use your body. Do not speak.

1. You worked hard all day. You are tired and your feet hurt. You don't like your job, and you don't make much money.

2. You are in a haunted house and you don't know how to get out. Suddenly you hear strange noises coming toward you.

3. You have just won first prize in an art contest. Everyone is applauding as you go up to receive your prize.

4. You are seventy years old. The day is bright and sunny, so you go for a walk. You meet some friends and go to the park.

Exercise B

Choose some classmates and act out your play without saying anything. Then talk about what you did.

7 Costumes and Props

Actors in a play wear costumes to show what kinds of characters they are playing. Sometimes, just one piece of costume is enough.

Exercise A

Talk about the kind of costume each of the following characters would wear.

1. A sheriff in the Old West
2. A very rich person
3. A doctor or a nurse
4. A captain of a boat

Exercise B

Write descriptions of the costumes that the characters in your play will wear.

How can you show where the story of your play takes place? You can use simple objects, such as a park bench, a bookcase, or a paper moon on a string. These objects are called *props*.

Exercise C

Write descriptions of the props you will use in your play.

Acting Out a Play

It takes many people to put on a play. One person cannot do it alone. Each job is important. Each job is necessary.

Exercise A

Choose one of the plays that someone in your class has written for Lessons 2 to 7. Then follow these steps.

1. Choose the actors who will play the characters in the play. The actors should read the story and memorize the words.
2. Choose one or more persons to find or make the props.
3. Choose one or more persons to find or make the costumes.
4. Practice the play a few times. Does everyone know his or her words? Are the costumes and props right?
5. When everything and everyone are ready, put on the play for the class.
6. If possible, put on the play for other classes in your school.

Exercise B

After the play, write about what you saw. What did you like in the play? What didn't you like? Tell why.

Plays About You

The main character in most stories and plays usually has to solve some kind of problem. Many of these problems are like the problems you have in real life. Some of them are easy to solve, and some are not. Think about a problem you have. Then imagine how you might solve it in a play.

Exercise A

Read each problem below and decide how you would solve it. Use the questions after each problem to help you. You might form groups in class. Then each group can put on a play to show how the problem was solved.

1. *Problem:* Kiri is a Native American girl. Her class is studying the history of the United States. Some of the books she reads do not talk fairly about the history of her people. She is disturbed.
   Questions: What should Kiri do? To whom should she speak? How can her class help her? How can she teach something to her class?

2. *Problem:* Everyone received an invitation to Bobby's party except Sam. He was hurt, but he didn't say anything. Melissa knew how Sam felt.
   Questions: What should Sam do? What should Melissa say to Bobby. What should she say to Sam? What should Bobby do?

3. *Problem:* Hanno wants to buy a portable radio. He is working after class to get the money. But he is so tired after work that he is not doing his homework. He is falling behind in class. His father says he has to quit his job.
Questions: How should Hanno solve this problem? What should his father say to him? What will Hanno say to his father? How can Hanno get his radio and still do his work in school?

Exercise B

Write out a problem and some questions to help solve it. Do not write your name on the paper. Have your classmates act out the problem and solve it.

If you were an actor in a play, would you have trouble reading the words below? Edit the words each character speaks so that they look like the example on page 179.

PAUL: What Happened? Where are we
Stan: "I don't know. it's so dark in here"
Carly: we're in some kind of tunnel look,
      there's a light at the other end
Paul: Let's go then i want to get out of here
      fast
STAN: "wait! what's that noise"
Carly: it's coming from over there.
Stan: Look, someone's coming toward us

EDITING EXERCISE

10 Using Your Language

Look at the verbs in the following sentences.

1. The Joneses <u>drive</u> a jeep.
2. They <u>drove</u> to Cape Cod last week.
3. They have <u>driven</u> there before.

The verb in sentence 1 shows present time. What time does the verb in sentence 2 show? Which verb is used with a helping word?

The word *drive* is used by itself to show present time. The word *drove* is used by itself to show past time. The word *driven* is used with a helping word.

drove   *did*
or   or
driven?   *done?*

wrote
or
written?

Talk about the verbs in these sentences.

1. I <u>write</u> good stories.
2. Ben <u>wrote</u> a ghost story.
3. She has <u>written</u> a long letter.

The word *write* is used by itself to show present time. The word *wrote* is used by itself to show past time. The word *written* is used with a helping word.

Talk about the verbs in these sentences.

1. I <u>do</u> my homework every night.
2. She <u>did</u> a complete cartwheel.
3. You have <u>done</u> it again!

The verb in sentence 1 shows present time. What time does the verb in sentence 2 show? Which verb is used with a helping word?

The word *do* is used by itself to show present time. The word *did* is used by itself to show past time. The word *done* is used with a helping word.

Exercise A

Write these sentences. Choose the correct word for the box in each one.

(did, done)	**1.** I have ☐ enough!
(wrote, written)	**2.** Irene ☐ it with a pen.
(drove, driven)	**3.** The bus ☐ down the street.
(wrote, written)	**4.** Raul had ☐ his name.
(drove, driven)	**5.** We have ☐ for ten hours.
(did, done)	**6.** Sammy ☐ the dishes.
(drove, driven)	**7.** The mosquitoes ☐ me crazy.
(wrote, written)	**8.** Her mother ☐ a novel.
(did, done)	**9.** She has ☐ all she can.
(wrote, written)	**10.** I have ☐ them a letter.

Exercise B

Use each of these verbs in a sentence of your own.

1. drove   **3.** wrote   **5.** did

2. driven   **4.** written   **6.** done

187

Can you imagine talking to a fish at the bottom of the sea? Can you imagine the fish talking back to you? That's exactly what happened to the boy in the following story. Read how he fed the fish. Then you will be asked to turn the story into a play.

FEEDING THE FISH

On a nice summer day, while standing by the water, a Little Boy met a Fish.

"Hello, Fish," he said.

"How do you do, Little Boy," said the Fish.

"I should like to see where you live," said the Little Boy.

"Hold on to my tail," said the Fish.

Down they went to the very bottom of the sea, the Boy holding on to the Fish's tail. On the bottom there were lots of fish, all kinds, colors, and shapes. They were all very polite, each one shaking hands with the Little Boy.

STRETCHING

"Would you like to meet the King Fish?" said the Fish.

"I should love to do that," said the Little Boy.

"But the rule is you must bring him a present."

"I have some cookies."

"Fine. He loves cookies," said the Fish.

The Little Boy went to see the King Fish. He was a very nice King Fish indeed. He was not grumpy and had pleasant things to say. He played with his toys very well and was quite willing to share. Just before he had to go, the Little Boy gave the King Fish his cookies.

YOUR IMAGINATION

The King said, "Oh, I do love cookies. Have you any more? Please give them to my friends." The Little Boy took out all the cookies and passed them to all the fish. They were eaten all up.

That night, when he got home, the Little Boy's Papa said, "What did you do today?"

"Oh," said the Little Boy, "I went to feed the fishes in the water."

"What a nice thing to do," said the Papa.

Writing a Play 11

A person who writes stories is an author. A person who writes plays is a playwright. Today you are going to get the chance to be a playwright. You will change the story "Feeding the Fish" into a play "Feeding the Fish."

Exercise A

Read the story carefully. Write down the different settings or places where the story takes place. Make a list of all the characters. Now you are ready to begin writing the play. Start writing the play by having the characters say what they said in the story. Continue in this way until the whole story is told.

Exercise B

Not many playwrights get the chance to put on their own plays. But you can have that chance! Choose different students to be the characters in the play. Help them learn to speak their lines the way you think the characters in the story would have said them. Show them how to do the action parts of the play. Choose other students to make whatever costumes and props are needed. Practice the play several times. Ask your teacher for a time to put on the play for the whole class. Just before the actors go on stage, say to them, "Break a leg." That is a saying actors use to wish each other good luck.

Reviewing
Your Skills

The page numerals after each heading show you where to look if you need help with this review.

Writing the Story of a Play (176)

Think of a story that you want to make into a play. It can be one you read, or you can make up your own. Then write a few sentences that tell what happens in the play. The sentences should answer these questions:

1. Which character has a problem to solve in the story?
2. What is the problem?
3. How does the character solve the problem?

Recognizing What the Characters Say (178–179)

Write the following conversation in the form of a play:

Betsy said, "I think someone is following us."
Nelson looked back and said, "I don't see anyone."
Betsy asked, "Don't you hear those footsteps?"

Costumes for a Play (182)

Write descriptions of the costumes that the following characters might wear.

1. A burglar
2. A scientist
3. An artist
4. A pirate
5. A construction worker
6. A cowhand

Props for a Play (182)

Describe the props you would use to show the following places in a play.

1. A ranch
2. A supermarket
3. An auditorium
4. A restaurant
5. A classroom
6. A beach
7. A living room
8. A desert
9. A forest
10. A laboratory

Solving Problems (184–185)

Choose a problem from below or one of your own. Write some questions to help solve it. Have your classmates act out the problem and solve it.

1. Kate takes good care of her bike. Her best friend wants to borrow it for a bike hike. Her best friend's bike was stolen when she left it unchained in the local playground. Kate is afraid her friend won't take care of Kate's bike either. But Kate doesn't want to hurt her friend's feelings.

2. The third graders are going on a boat ride. Brian can't swim and is afraid of the water. He doesn't want to go on the trip but doesn't want anyone to know why.

3. Marika's mother has just lost her job. Marika's birthday is one week away. Marika wants a new bike.

4. Jack's cousin is visiting from another state. He speaks with a slightly different accent. Jack's friends make fun of his cousin's accent.

Writing the Story of a Play

Think of a story that you want to make into a play. It can be one you read, or you can make up your own. Then write a few sentences that tell what happens in the play. The sentences should answer these questions:

1. Which character has a problem to solve in the story?
2. What is the problem?
3. How does the character solve the problem?

Recognizing What the Characters Say

Write the following conversation in the form of a play:

Brad asked, "Do you like this cartoon I drew?"
Chris answered, "Well, I'm not sure I understand it."
Brad sighed, "But don't you think it's funny anyway?"
Chris said, "Why don't we ask Jill?"
Brad answered, "That's a good idea."

Costumes for a Play

Write descriptions of the costumes that the following characters might wear.

1. A king
2. A farmer
3. A soldier
4. A plumber
5. A salesclerk
6. A spy

Props for a Play

Describe the props you would use to show the following places in a play:

1. A castle
2. An outdoor market
3. A playground
4. An office
5. A ferry
6. A cabin
7. A circus
8. A kitchen
9. A lighthouse
10. A laundromat

Solving Problems

Choose a problem from below or one of your own. Write some questions to help solve it. Have your classmates act out the problem and solve it.

1. Three friends often played games together. The same friend always won. The other two friends wondered if their friend cheated.

2. Irene is staying at the home of a friend. The first morning, her friend's mother serves Irene hot cereal for breakfast. Irene doesn't like hot cereal.

3. Dave has just finished washing the dishes. It's his brother Bob's job to dry them. Bob says that he's busy doing homework and that Dave should finish the job.

4. Rita is hurrying to school. She doesn't want to be late. She notices a small boy wandering in the street. The child is sobbing that he's lost.

5. Joy finds a stray dog. The dog is wearing a license tag. Joy would like to keep the dog.

Skills Checkup

Writing Statements and Questions (17–18)

A. Write each group of words below as a statement:

1. the postcard is from Aunt June
2. the door is locked
3. that is my lunch bag
4. the library is on Front Street

B. Write each group of words in Part A as a question.

Writing Titles (41)

Write these titles correctly:

1. my favorite game
2. the grasshopper
3. all about rocks
4. my favorite sound
5. the bear in the cave
6. saving for something special

Writing Plural Nouns (62–63)

Write the plural form of each of the following singular nouns:

1. buzz　　2. patch　　3. shoe　　4. fox　　5. chance

Writing Possessive Nouns (64–65)

Write each sentence below. Use the possessive form of the noun at the left for the box in each sentence.

(puppy)　　**1.** The ☐ bone is buried.
(artist)　　**2.** The ☐ painting is colorful.
(mother)　　**3.** I'm going to my ☐ office.
(friend)　　**4.** My ☐ bike is next to mine.

Writing a Friendly Letter (88–96)

Put the five parts of the friendly letter in order. Write them correctly as parts of the same letter.

1. your friend
2. dear greg
3. 893 new london road
   glenview illinois 60025
   may 5 19--
4. eric
5. thank you for thinking of me on my birthday it was a great day mom and dad took me to the zoo then we ate dinner in a restaurant your card was waiting when i got home it was so nice of you to send it i hope you can visit me very soon

Using Alphabetical Order (118–119)

Write the numerals 1 to 12 on your paper. Then write the following words in alphabetical order.

aunt	purple	window
kangaroo	next	meadow
crash	design	finish
sled	tunnel	target

Making Verbs Show Time (150–151)

Use each verb below in two sentences. In the first sentence, show present time. In the second sentence, show past time.

1. play
2. work
3. dance
4. call
5. ask
6. push

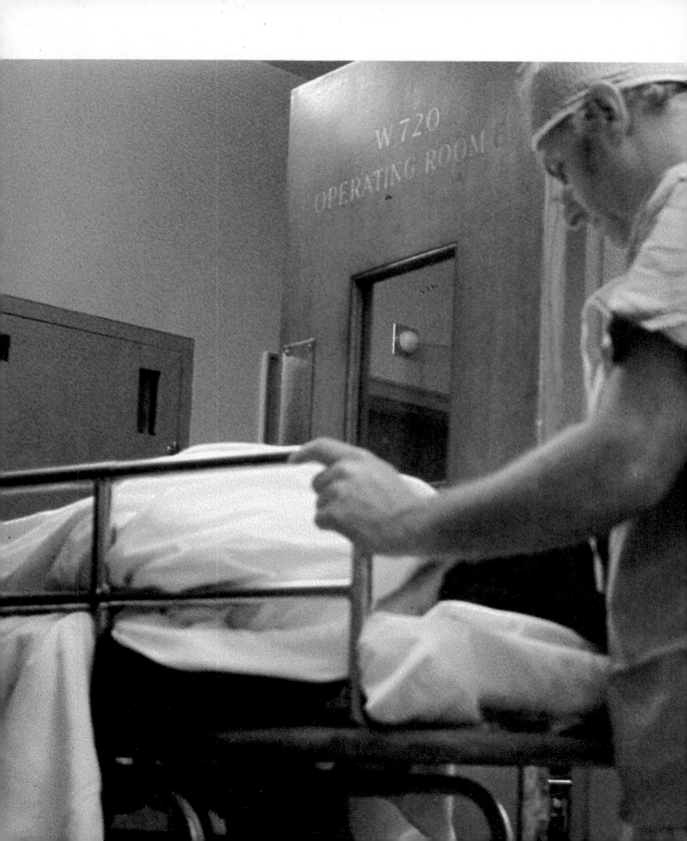

Writing Paragraphs

COMPOSITION Recognizing Paragraphs
Paragraphs That Tell a
    Story
Paragraphs That Describe
Paragraphs That Explain
Paragraphs That Give
    Directions
Words That Help
    Paragraph Order

MECHANICS Paragraph Indention

USAGE Using *went* or *gone; ate* or
    eaten; took or *taken*

In this unit, you will work with
sentences that belong together. Then you
will meet a grandparent who had a most
unusual classmate.

1 What Is a Paragraph?

Read the following group of sentences about the picture on pages 198–199:

1. The hospital was very busy. Doctors and nurses in white uniforms hurried through the hallways. Two aides wheeled a person on a table into an operating room. A young boy hobbled by on crutches with his leg in a cast. Two police officers brought in a woman in a wheelchair. A baby in its mother's arms was crying loudly.

Now read this group of sentences:

2. There are many hospitals in the city. My grandmother lives near a big hospital. The people in the hospital work very hard. The subway and the bus stop near the hospital.

Which group of sentences is a paragraph? The questions below will help you find out.

Read the first group of sentences again.

1. What does the first group of sentences tell about?

2. Are all the sentences about the busy hospital?

A paragraph is a group of sentences that tell about one thing. The first group of sentences is a paragraph. The first sentence of a paragraph is indented. If you don't know what *indented* means, look at the first line of this paragraph.

Read the second group of sentences again before answering the questions on the next page.

1. What four things does the second group of sentences tell about?
2. Is the second group of sentences a paragraph?

The second group of sentences is not a paragraph. It starts off with a sentence about hospitals. Then it tells about Grandmother, about people who work hard, and about subways and buses.

Exercise A

Read each group of sentences. Decide whether each one is a paragraph.

1. Some animals at the Bronx Zoo do not live in cages. They roam a large outdoor area called Wild Asia. Visitors can hardly believe that they are in a big city zoo. Hidden fences take the place of cages. The animals look as though they are at home in the jungle or on the plains.

2. My grandmother taught me how to find weather signs in the sky. Clouds that look like fluffy cotton usually mean good weather. Very tall clouds that spread at the top often bring showers. Heavy, dark clouds that cover the sky usually mean rain or snow.

Exercise B

Find an interesting paragraph in one of your textbooks. Be ready to tell why it is a paragraph.

2 Sentences That Belong Together

The one thing that a paragraph tells about is called the *main idea*. A sentence at the beginning of the paragraph usually tells the main idea. Sometimes a sentence at the end of the paragraph tells the main idea. What is the main idea of the paragraph on page 200? Which sentence tells the main idea?

Exercise A

Read the following paragraphs. What is the main idea in each one? Which sentence tells the main idea?

1. Ralph cleaned up his room on Saturday morning. First, he picked up his clothes and put them away. Then he collected his toys and arranged them on the shelves. He made his bed, dusted the furniture, and swept the floor. Finally, he called his mom and showed her what he had done.

2. The bed she slept in was hard and lumpy. The flies and mosquitoes bit and bothered her. The food was terrible. The lake was muddy. It rained for three days. Most of the girls in her tent were homesick. Margaret was not having a good time at camp.

Every sentence in a paragraph should tell something about the main idea. If a sentence does not tell about the main idea, it does not belong in the paragraph.

Exercise B

Read the paragraphs in Exercise A again. Talk about how the sentences in each one tell about the main idea.

Exercise C

Write the following group of sentences so that they are a paragraph. Leave out any sentence that does not tell about the main idea. Then write a first sentence that states the main idea.

Some dogs, like the Saint Bernard, are big and heavy. The Saint Bernard's coat is usually white and shaggy with brown patches. I don't like big dogs. Some dogs are long and low, like the dachshund. The dachshund has short brown hair. Some dogs are tall and thin, like the greyhound. The greyhound's legs are long and skinny, and its back is curved like a hill. My uncle owns two dogs.

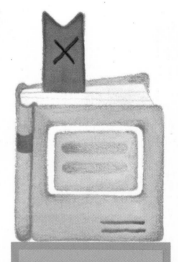

Facts About Language

As language grows, people put words together to make new words: *bookmark, bookends, bookshelf, bookcase.*

Exercise D

Each sentence tells a main idea for a paragraph. Choose one of the sentences and write it. Then write several sentences that tell about the main idea you have chosen.

1. There are lots of things to do by yourself.
2. Lenny made a Valentine's Day card.
3. Travel by train (or bus) can be fun.
4. Houses are made of different materials.

3 Paragraphs That Tell a Story

Some stories can be told in one paragraph. But sometimes you may have to use two or more paragraphs to tell a longer story. How do you know when to begin a new paragraph in a story? Exercise A will help you find out.

Exercise A

The following paragraph is the beginning of a story. It should be divided into two paragraphs. Tell where you would begin the second paragraph. Be ready to tell why.

It was dark when Mary got to the lake. She found the shovels under the porch and quietly dragged them down to the shore. No one saw her as she got into the boat and rowed away. When she got to the island, she hid the boat with some branches. Then she dragged the shovels up the hill and entered the cave. She was now ready to get to work.

Did you begin a new paragraph with the sentence "When she got to the island, she hid the boat with some branches"? Each time you tell another part of a story, begin a new paragraph.

When you write a story, the paragraphs should be in the right order. The events in each paragraph should also be in the right order.

Follow these guidelines for writing paragraphs:

1. Write a sentence that tells the main idea.

2. Write sentences that tell about the main idea.

3. Begin a new paragraph each time you tell another part of a story.

Exercise B

The following story is all mixed up. Write the sentences in each paragraph in the right order. Then write the three paragraphs in the right order.

When he got home, he told his mom all about his new friends. He was so tired that he quickly fell asleep. Then his mother asked him about his teachers. At 9 o'clock he went to his room and plopped down on the bed. After eating, he did his homework, watched some TV, and had a snack.

Today was Alex's first day at his new school. Then he rushed out the door with his books and lunchbox. He jumped out of bed and got dressed quickly. He had to run to catch the bus. He gulped down his breakfast in two minutes flat.

When he got to school, Alex didn't know any of the children. During recess, he met Tom and Jerry. By the end of the day, he knew most of the boys and girls in his class. They asked him to join them in a game of stickball. In his first class, he met Joe, Sylvia, and Oscar.

Paragraphs That Describe

Sometimes a paragraph in a story gives a word picture of a person, place, or thing. The word picture is called a *description*. The following paragraph describes a person from the Old West.

An old leather hat sat on top of his black shaggy hair. Around his neck he wore a red bandanna. His shirt was gray and torn, and his vest had fringes on it. Over his jeans he wore a pair of chaps with silver studs down the sides. The spurs on his dirty, scuffed boots jangled as he walked. He was a real cowhand.

Exercise A

Read the paragraph above again. Then answer the following questions and talk about your answers in class.

1. Which sentence tells the main idea of the paragraph?
2. How do words like *old, leather,* and *red* give you a picture of the cowboy?
3. What is described first? What is described last?
4. How does describing the cowboy from head to feet help you picture what he looked like?

Follow the guidelines on the next page when you write a description.

1. Use words that give a word picture of the person, place, or thing you are describing.

2. Write your description in some kind of order that helps the reader picture what you are describing.

Exercise B

Talk about describing words in the following sentences. Tell how each one gives a word picture of what is being described.

1. The dark blue grapes were spotted with brown and tasted bitter.
2. Leona coughed loudly as the thick smoke burned her throat and stung her eyes.

Exercise C

Study the picture below. Then write a describing paragraph about it.

5 Paragraphs That Explain

When you tell someone how to do something, you are explaining. When you explain something, it is important to give all the steps. It is also important to give the steps in the right order.

Read this explanation of how to scramble eggs:

Break two eggs into a bowl and add a teaspoon of water. Beat the eggs with a fork. Put a pan on the stove to get it hot. Put some butter in the hot pan. Pour the eggs into the pan and stir them with a fork. When the eggs are done, slide them onto a warm plate.

Answer these questions about the paragraph:

1. How many steps are in the paragraph?
2. Are the steps given one at a time?
3. Which steps tell how to get the eggs ready?
4. Which steps are about heating the pan?
5. Which steps tell how to cook the eggs?
6. Are the steps given in the right order?

Suppose that in the middle of explaining how to scramble eggs, the writer told how he or she felt about scrambled eggs:

I like scrambled eggs. They are my favorite breakfast food.

Do feelings about eggs help explain how to scramble eggs? A paragraph that explains should tell facts only. It should not tell feelings.

Follow these guidelines when you write a paragraph that explains:

1. Give all the important steps.

2. Give the steps one at a time.

3. Give the steps in the right order.

4. Tell facts only, not feelings.

Exercise

Write a paragraph that explains how to do something. The topics below may give you an idea. Be sure to follow the guidelines at the top of the page.

1. A favorite game   **2.** A favorite hobby

Edit the paragraph below. Find the sentence that does not belong. Find the step that is out of order.

Unfold a paper clip. Bend one end up carefully to make a cradle. Paper clips come in handy. Put a second clip on the cradle. Fill a small bowl with water. With the cradle, gently place the paper clip on the water. It should float in the bowl without sinking.

EDITING EXERCISE

Another Kind of Explanation

A paragraph that tells how to get from one place to another is also an explaining paragraph. The directions must be clear and simple. Each step must be in the right order.

 Exercise A

Suppose you invited your parents to a science fair in your classroom. Could you give them directions for finding your room? Discuss these questions:

1. Which door do you use to come into school?
2. Which direction does that door face—north, south, east, or west?
3. Which way do you turn when you get inside—left or right?
4. Do you have to go upstairs or downstairs?
5. Is your room marked with a numeral or with your teacher's name?

Follow these guidelines for giving directions:

1. Give the starting point of your directions (the front door of the school).

2. Use words that help make your directions clear *(north, south, left, right, upstairs, downstairs).*

3. Give other information that may help (how your classroom is marked).

Exercise B

Write the directions you discussed in Exercise A. Remember to follow the guidelines for giving directions.

Exercise C

Here are two sets of directions for getting from the school shown on the map below to a house on Jackson Avenue. Which directions do you think it would be easier to follow? Be ready to tell why.

1. When you go out the front door of your school, you will be on Fourth Street. Turn to the right and cross Adams Avenue. Walk one block to Jackson Avenue. Cross Jackson Avenue. I live in the tall building on the corner of Jackson Avenue and Fourth Street. The address is 624 Jackson Avenue. Our apartment is on the third floor. It is Apartment 302.

2. I live at the corner of Jackson Avenue and Fourth Street. Jackson Avenue is just one block from school. I live in Apartment 302.

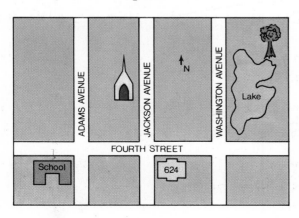

7 Words That Build Good Paragraphs

Some paragraphs tell stories. Some paragraphs describe. Some paragraphs explain. But all paragraphs have one thing in common. Do you know what that one thing is? The sentences in each and every paragraph must be in the right order.

Different kinds of paragraphs have different kinds of order. A paragraph that tells a story is usually arranged by time. Words like *later, yesterday,* and *after dinner* can help you to show the time order of a story.

Exercise A

Talk about the words that show the time order in the following story.

This morning when I woke up, I still felt tired. I lay in bed for a few minutes. Then I got up, washed, and got dressed. After fixing my bed, I made some toast and tea for breakfast. Later that morning, I did some work in the garden. At one o'clock, my friend Sandy came by and we went for a walk in the park. That night my dad and I went to a horror movie.

Exercise B

Write a short story in one or two paragraphs. Use words that show the time order.

A paragraph that describes usually uses words that show where things are. Words like *on the left* and *outside* show where things are.

Exercise C

Write a list of words that can help you to show where things are in a description.

Exercise D

Write a paragraph that describes a person, place, or thing. Use words that show where things are in the description.

A paragraph that explains uses different words to show order. The most often used words are *first, second, next, then, last,* and *finally*.

Exercise E

Write a paragraph that explains how to make something. Use words that show order.

Exercise F

Decide what kind of paragraph you would write about each of the following. Then choose one and write the paragraph.

1. How to make a paper airplane
2. Adventures in outer space
3. A modern skyscraper

Using Your Language

Look at the verbs in the following sentences:

1. They <u>went</u> to another camp.
2. She has <u>gone</u> there twice before.

Both verbs show past time. Which verb is used with a helping word?

**went
or
gone?**

The verb *went* is used by itself to show past time. The verb *gone* is used with a helping word.

Now look at the verbs in these sentences:

1. You <u>ate</u> all the doughnuts.
2. We have <u>eaten</u> already.

Both verbs show past time. Which verb is used with a helping word?

**ate
or
eaten?**

The verb *ate* is used by itself to show past time. The verb *eaten* is used with a helping word.

Remember that there is no such word as "et." Say: "I ate an apple" and "I have eaten an apple," not "I et an apple."

214

Exercise A

Write each sentence. Use a form of the verb at the left for the box. Your sentence should show past time.

(go)   **1.** I ☐ to bed early.
(eat)   **2.** She has ☐ here before.
(eat)   **3.** The dog ☐ my shoe.
(go)   **4.** The guests have ☐ home.
(eat)   **5.** A worm has ☐ this apple.

Look at the verbs in these sentences:

1. The test <u>took</u> three hours!
2. You have <u>taken</u> enough of my time.

Both verbs show past time. Which verb is used with a helping word?

The verb *took* is used by itself to show past time. The verb *taken* is used with a helping word.

took
or
taken?

Exercise B

Write each sentence. Use a form of the verb at the left for the box. Your sentence should show past time.

(take) **1.** I ☐ my own temperature.
(go)   **2.** The road ☐ under the bridge.
(eat)   **3.** Who has ☐ my spinach?
(take) **4.** Ken has ☐ some photos.
(take) **5.** What has ☐ you so long?

215

In this unit, you learned about paragraphs in a story. Now you will stretch your imagination and read some paragraphs about a grandfather who knew someone called Jack.

STRINGBEANS

"I don't want any beans," said Teddy, pushing his plate away.

"Teddy," said Mommy, "eat your food."

"I like stringbeans," said Nora, biting into one of her beans.

"Of course, you do," said Daddy. "Everyone likes stringbeans."

"No," said Teddy. "Not me!"

"Well," said Grandpa. "I can remember a time when I had to eat too many beans. It was a long time ago, when I was a little boy about your age. I lived in the country then. Next door to my house, there was a woman and her son. You may have heard about him. His name was Jack."

"Jack? I don't know anyone named Jack," said Teddy.

STRETCHING

"Well," said Grandpa. "He was a lazy, unpleasant fellow. I never liked him too much. But let me tell you what happened one day. Jack's mother needed money to buy some food, so she told Jack to take the cow to town and sell it. Only instead of selling it, he traded it away to a man in exchange for a handful of colored beans."

"*That* Jack!" shouted Teddy and Nora. "Grandpa, did you really know *that* Jack who had the beanstalk?"

"I sure did," answered Grandpa. "I thought you might have heard about him. Well, Jack brought home those colored beans, and his mother was so angry, she just threw them out the window and sent Jack upstairs to bed. In the morning, when I was leaving for school, I saw an enormous thing growing outside of Jack's house."

"The beanstalk!" cried Teddy and Nora with delight.

"Yes, that's right," said Grandpa. "I knocked on Jack's door and asked if he wanted to walk to school with me. But Jack said he was going to stay home and climb to the top of his beanstalk."

"To the giant!" shouted Nora.

"What happened next?" asked Teddy.

YOUR IMAGINATION

"Well," said Grandpa. "The teacher was furious with Jack. He was a bad student. He never paid attention in class or did his homework. And now he was playing hooky as well. I was sure he would get into trouble. But when I came home from school that afternoon, there was Jack holding a hen that could lay golden eggs. Everyone thought he was wonderful. When the teacher came to complain to Jack's mother, Jack gave her a golden egg."

"And the next day, Jack stayed home from school again and climbed the beanstalk for a second time, and he brought back —"

"A bag of gold!" shouted Teddy.

"Right!" said Grandpa. "And the next day, he stayed home from school again. This time he got a golden harp. Only this time the giant started to follow him down the beanstalk. So when he reached the bottom, he shouted to his mother to bring him an axe."

"And she did, and she chopped down the beanstalk," said Nora.

"Wrong!" said Grandpa. "All those books are wrong! Jack's mother wasn't home. She was out spending the gold pieces. But luckily I had just returned from school. I ran and got my axe, and I chopped the beanstalk down for him."

"Oh, Grandpa. That's wonderful!" breathed Nora.

"Did you see the giant fall?" asked Teddy.

"Of course," said Grandpa. "They may not write about me in the story, but I was there."

"Then what happened?" asked Nora.

"Well, we buried the giant. He made an enormous hole where he landed, and we filled it in with dirt. As for the beanstalk, it had so many beans on it that we picked for three weeks without stopping. We had stringbeans for dinner every night for a month. And stringbean soup for lunch and even stringbean cereal for breakfast in the morning."

"That was a long, long time ago, but I still think of it whenever I have stringbeans for dinner," said Grandpa.

"Teddy, where are your beans?" asked Grandma.

"Did you throw them on the floor?" asked Nora.

Teddy looked down at his plate. He looked under the table. Then he smiled. "I guess I ate them," he said.

JOHANNA HURWITZ

Do you believe that Grandpa really knew Jack? He seemed to know a lot about what happened to the beanstalk. Now you will have a chance to s-t-r-e-t-c-h your imagination and tell the real story behind an old story we all know . . . or think we know.

Exercise

Choose one of the stories pictured below. Pretend that you were actually present at the time the story took place. Tell what really happened.

Reviewing Your Skills

The page numerals after each heading show you where to look if you need help with this review.

Correcting a Storytelling Paragraph (202–205)

The following sentences are mixed up. Write the sentences in the right order. Leave out the sentence that does not belong.

Sandy lived with his family in London, the largest city in England. The dog was almost as tall as Sandy, and Sandy held on to King's collar when they took a walk. King was Sandy's best friend and constant playmate. Sandy would hold King's collar and throw back his head to listen to the giant booms. Sandy and King often walked to the square to listen to the big clock strike the hour. Many cities have big clocks.

Writing a Describing Paragraph (206–207, 212–213)

Choose one of the following. Write a describing paragraph about it. Choose your words carefully and arrange them in a certain order.

1. wind
2. a campfire
3. popping corn
4. an athlete
5. a flower
6. caramels
7. a piece of paper
8. a magician
9. an animal
10. rain

Writing an Explaining Paragraph (208–209)

Write a paragraph that explains how to do something. Choose a topic from below or use one of your own.

1. A favorite sport
2. A favorite do-it-yourself project
3. A favorite hobby
4. A favorite recipe
5. A favorite place

Writing Different Kinds of Paragraphs (204–209)

Decide what kind of paragraph you would write about each of the following. Then choose one and write the paragraph.

1. How to plan a birthday party
2. A scary moment
3. A mosquito

Writing Directions in Order (210–211)

Write in correct order these directions for getting to the library from the school by bus.

1. When you get off the bus, walk to the corner of 24 Street and Michigan Street and turn right on 24 Street.
2. The bus stops in front of school on Michigan Street.
3. When you walk out of school, do not cross the street.
4. Take the bus to West 24 Street.
5. The library will be on your right at the end of the block.

Testing Your Skills

Correcting a Storytelling Paragraph

The following sentences are mixed up. Write the sentences in the right order. Leave out the sentence that does not belong.

When Nina woke up early Saturday morning, the snow was falling hard. A snow-covered street looks pretty. The wind was howling. Nina's mother had promised to take her to see a new movie. Would the snow spoil their outing? The little strip of road that she could see from her apartment window was buried under a blanket of snow. Nina hoped not.

Writing a Describing Paragraph

Choose one of the following. Write a describing paragraph about it. Choose your words carefully and arrange them in a certain order.

1. a fire siren
2. a rainbow
3. a sandy beach
4. sunrise
5. fog
6. squirrels
7. bread baking in the oven
8. shadows
9. a box of crayons
10. a summer day
11. pigeons
12. a windmill

Writing an Explaining Paragraph

Write a paragraph that explains how to make something or how something is done. Choose a topic from below or use one of your own.

1. How to make a terrarium
2. How to care for tropical fish
3. How to play Chinese checkers
4. How to make potato prints
5. How to make your own secret code

Writing Different Kinds of Paragraphs

Decide what kind of paragraph you would write about each of the following. Then choose one and write the paragraph.

1. How to identify animal tracks
2. A good friend
3. Learning the hard way

Writing Directions in Order

Write in correct order these directions for finding the drugstore from your school.

1. The drugstore is at the corner of Sixth Avenue and Moore Street.
2. On Sixth Avenue, walk one block to Moore Street.
3. On Webster Street, walk two blocks to Sixth Avenue and turn left.
4. When you leave the front door of school, turn left.
5. Walk one block to Webster Street and turn right.

Writing Statements and Questions (17–18)

A. Write each group of words below as a statement:

1. this melon is ripe
2. ellie has found my pen
3. carol is interested in science
4. the circus is coming to town
5. you are wearing a costume

B. Write each group of words in Part A as a question.

Writing Titles (41)

Write these titles correctly:

1. a stitch in time
2. helpful insects
3. out on the fire escape
4. in a hurry
5. my first pet

6. my favorite color
7. a cry for help
8. my friend and i
9. learning to swim
10. a busy ant

Finding Nouns in the Subject and the Predicate (58–59)

Write each sentence below. Draw a slash mark between the subject and the predicate. Then circle each noun you find in the subject and the predicate.

1. The sun melted the snow.
2. The pupils have new books.
3. Our neighbor waxed her car.
4. The guitarist played several songs.
5. The audience cheered the acrobats.

Writing a Friendly Letter (88–95)

Write this letter in correct form. Be sure to use capital letters and punctuation marks in the right places.

369 planter drive hilo hawaii 96720 july 10 19-- dear pat i am having an exciting vacation in hawaii my friend is teaching me how to ride a surfboard the good surfers can stand on the very front of the surfboard i still have to stand near the back maybe i will get better before it is time to come home your friend joe

Using Alphabetical Order (118–119)

Write the numerals 1 to 10 on your paper. Then write the following words in alphabetical order.

pencil	magazine	carnival	elevator	wagon
dream	newspaper	furnace	roof	fable

Making Verbs Show Time (150–151)

Use each verb below in two sentences. In the first sentence, show present time. In the second sentence, show past time.

1. bake **3.** walk **5.** blame
2. clean **4.** visit **6.** use

Recognizing What the Characters Say (178–179)

Write the following conversation in the form of a play.

Gloria asked, "Where are you going?"
Sharon said, "We're going to watch the Fourth of July fireworks."
Dave added, "Why don't you join us?"

Using Facts

COMPOSITION	Knowing Facts and Opinions
	Asking Questions
	Taking Notes
	Making a Plan
	Writing a Report
MECHANICS	Checking a Report
SPEAKING	Reading a Report to the Class
LISTENING	Listening to a Report
USAGE	Using *knew* and *known; grew* and *grown; saw* and *seen*

In this unit, you will learn how to put facts into a report. Then you will use your imagination to write about a dinosaur that talks.

1 What Are Facts?

How much is 8 plus 5? Who was the first President of the United States? In what city will you find the Golden Gate Bridge? The answers to all three questions are facts.

> Fact: 8 plus 5 is 13.
> Fact: George Washington was the first President of the United States.
> Fact: The Golden Gate Bridge is in San Francisco.

Can each of these statements be proved? A fact is a statement that can be proved.

Now read the statements below. Are they facts?

1. Math is very easy.
2. Reading about Presidents is interesting.
3. San Francisco is fun to visit.

Each of these statements tells what someone thinks about something. Something that someone only thinks is true is not a fact. It is an opinion.

In this unit, you will be using facts to write a report. The exercise below will help you find out if you know the difference between a fact and an opinion.

Exercise

Tell whether each of the following statements is a fact or an opinion.

1. There are 100 centimeters in a meter.
2. The metric system is the best system.
3. The earth revolves around the sun.
4. Summer is the best time of the year.
5. Everyone likes baseball.
6. Baseball is popular in the United States.
7. San Juan is the capital of Puerto Rico.
8. San Juan has one of the best harbors in the world.
9. Moon travel is exciting.
10. The moon is 4.6 billion years old.

2 Asking Questions

What is a reporter? What does a reporter do? Flora is a reporter for her school paper. She is always asking questions. Some people say that she asks too many questions. But Flora says that it's her job to ask questions. A reporter has to know facts so that he or she can write a report. One of the best ways to learn facts is by asking questions.

Reporters must report their facts carefully. They must not say that something is a fact unless they have proof that it is so.

 Exercise A

Pretend you are a reporter for your school paper. You have to write a report about each of the events below. Write at least three questions that you would ask in order to learn the facts about each event. Talk about your questions in class.

1. A teacher won a prize in a contest.
2. One of the clubs at school had a picnic.
3. The zoo has a new animal.
4. Another school in the city is moving to a new location.
5. An empty building was destroyed last night.

With what kind of words did many of the questions you wrote for Exercise A begin? A good news reporter tells all the important facts by answering the questions "Who?" "What?" "Where?" "When?" and "How?"

A report written in class can tell about something that happened. It can tell about a person or a group of persons. It can tell about a place. Or it can tell about an object or thing. A good report written in class tells all the important facts that answer the questions "Who?" "What?" "Where?" "When?" and "How?" What you write about in a report is called the *topic*.

Exercise B

Write the headings *Happening, Person, Place,* and *Thing* across the top of your paper. Under each heading write at least two topics that you might write a report about. Then talk about your topics in class.

Exercise C

Choose one topic under each heading in Exercise B and write it on your paper. Then write at least three questions that you would ask to learn the facts about each topic. Talk about your topics and questions in class.

Exercise D

Look at the questions you wrote in Exercise C. Talk about how you might find answers to those questions.

Facts About Language

People use different words for the same thing. Which do you say: *soda* or *pop*? *couch* or *sofa*? *faucet* or *tap*?

233

3 Finding Facts

What ideas for finding answers did you talk about in Exercise D on page 233? There are several different ways to find facts. You can ask someone who knows the facts. You can read a book, magazine, or newspaper that tells the facts. You can also learn the facts yourself. If you want to know how many boys and girls are in your class, for example, you can count them yourself.

The librarian may be able to answer some of your questions. But you will have to read books to find most of the facts you are looking for. Ask the librarian to help you to find these books.

Exercise A

Look at the questions you wrote in Exercise C on page 233. Tell where you would find the facts that answer the questions.

The answers to your questions in Exercise C are the facts that you will use to write your report. As you find the answer to each question, write it in your own words. These written answers are called *notes.* They will help you when you write your report. A note can be one word, a group of words, or a whole sentence. Read the notes on the next page for a report on cactuses. Then study the guidelines carefully.

1. Where do cactuses grow?
in dry deserts all over the world
along the shores of oceans and lakes

2. What are cactuses good for?
for their juices
for their fruit
for their helpful drugs and medicines

Follow these guidelines when you take notes for a report:

1. Write the answers to each question you want to answer.

2. Write the answers in your own words.

3. Use sentences only if you want to.

Exercise B

Read the paragraphs below. Then take notes for part of a report on the right light for house plants. Your notes should answer these questions: (1) Where can bright light be found? (2) Where can low light be found?

Bright light can be found in rooms with windows that face east, west, and south. Plants that are placed three feet or less from these windows will get bright light. Bright light can also be found in the center of a sunny room.

Low light can be found in a room without windows or with windows that face north. Low light can also be found in the center of a room with covered windows.

4 Planning Your Report

Before you write your report, you should have a plan. Your plan will show the ideas you are going to write about. It will also show the order of the facts that tell about your ideas. You will usually have two main ideas in your report. Sometimes you will have more than two. Look at the following plan for a report on cactuses.

The Helpful Cactus
I. Where cactuses grow
   A. In dry desert areas
   B. Along the shores of oceans and lakes
II. How cactuses are helpful
   A. For their juice
   B. For their fruit
   C. For their medicine

Exercise A

Answer the following questions about the plan above.

1. How many main ideas are there in the plan? What are they? How are they marked?
2. How many facts tell about the first main idea? What are they? How are they marked?
3. How many facts tell about the second main idea? What are they? How are they marked?

The main ideas in your plan should be in a certain order. The facts that tell about each main idea should be in a certain order. Follow these guidelines for putting your ideas in order:

1. Your title should tell what the report is about.

2. Roman numeral I should mark an important idea.

3. The facts under the first important idea should tell interesting things about that idea.

4. Roman numeral II should mark a second important idea.

5. The facts under the second idea should tell interesting things about that idea.

 Exercise B

Follow the steps below to write a plan for a report.

1. Choose a topic about an event, a person, a place, or a thing. If you wish, use one of the topics you chose for Exercise C on page 233.

2. Write two questions about your topic.

3. Find the facts that answer the questions and write your notes.

4. Write a plan like the one on page 236.
   a. Use a Roman numeral and a period to mark each main idea.
   b. Use a capital letter and a period to mark each fact about a main idea.

5 Writing Your Report

A report is made up of two or more paragraphs that tell about one topic. Each paragraph tells one main idea about the topic.

A plan for a report shows what the main idea of each paragraph is. It shows in what order the paragraphs are arranged. A plan also shows the facts that tell about each main idea.

You know how to write paragraphs. You also know how to write a plan for a report. Now you are ready to think about writing a report.

Here are some guidelines for writing a report:

1. Write a first sentence that states the main idea of the first paragraph.

2. Write one sentence for each fact that tells about the first main idea.

3. Write a first sentence that states the main idea of the second paragraph.

4. Write one sentence for each fact that tells about the second main idea.

5. Write a last sentence that makes your two paragraphs go together.

 Exercise

You are now ready to write your report. Use the plan you wrote for Exercise B on page 237. Follow the guidelines above.

Choosing a Title

The person who planned the report on page 236 decided at first to call the report "Cactuses." Does a main idea come to mind when you read that title? Why is the title "The Helpful Cactus" better?

Follow these guidelines for writing a title:

1. Choose a title that tells what your report is about.

2. Choose a title that will make the reader want to read your report.

3. Write the first, last, and all important words with a capital letter.

Exercise A

Write a title for the report you wrote for the exercise on page 238. Follow the guidelines above.

The title is an important part of a report. So are the first and last sentences.

Exercise B

Read the report you wrote for the exercise on page 238. Does the first sentence make the reader want to finish the report? Does the last sentence pull the report together? Work on your first and last sentences until they are the best you can write.

7 Checking Your Report

When you check your report, think about what you wrote and how you wrote it. Use the following questions to help you.

What You Wrote

1. Is your title interesting?

2. Does your opening sentence make the reader want to finish the report?

3. Are the paragraphs in the right order?

4. Does the first sentence of each paragraph state the main idea of the paragraph?

5. Do the other sentences in each paragraph tell about the main idea?

6. Are the sentences in each paragraph in the right order?

7. Does your last sentence help pull your report together?

How You Wrote It

1. Is each paragraph indented?

2. Did you spell all the words correctly?

3. Did you use capital letters where they belong?

4. Did you use commas, periods, and question marks where they belong? Use the Handbook if you need help.

Read your report. Follow these steps:

1. Ask yourself the first group of questions on page 240. Make any changes that are needed.
2. Ask yourself the second group of questions on page 240. Make any changes that are needed.
3. Rewrite your corrected report neatly.

Read the report below. Is the title interesting? Is there a last sentence that pulls the paragraph together? Did the writer use capital letters and punctuation marks where they belong? Write the report correctly.

names of places

Some places in america are named after famous people. Washington, D.C., is named after the first President of the United states. the famous Native American athlete Jim thorpe gave his name to a town in pennsylvania

Other places have names that describe where they are located. Salt Lake City, utah, sits on the shore of the Great Salt Lake. Level Land, texas, is a great flat plain in the western part of texas.

EDITING EXERCISE

⑧ Reading Your Report

After you write your report, you will want to read it to the class. But before you do, read it over again. Make sure you know how to pronounce each word correctly. Practice reading out loud to hear if you are speaking loudly, slowly, and clearly enough.

When you get ready to read your report, follow these guidelines:

1. Stand up straight and don't move around too much.

2. Hold your paper so that you can look at your classmates as you read.

3. Read loudly enough for everyone to hear.

4. Speak slowly and clearly.

5. Pause briefly between the title and the opening sentence.

6. Pause briefly between paragraphs.

7. When you finish reading, ask for questions from the class.

8. If you can't answer a question, tell where someone might find the answer.

 Exercise

Read your report to the class. Be ready to answer questions.

Listening to a Report

Listening to reports is an easy way to learn. You spend much of your time in school and at home listening to what other people are saying. But do you really know how to listen? There are different ways of listening. Sometimes you listen to learn new ideas. Sometimes you listen to remember something you already know. And sometimes you listen just for fun.

The following questions will help you write guidelines for listening:

1. How do you get ready to listen?
2. Do you pay attention to the speaker?
3. Do you think along with the speaker?
4. Do you try to pick out the speaker's main ideas?
5. Do you remember things in the order in which you hear them?
6. Are you polite to the person who is speaking?

Exercise

Make a list of things you should remember when you are listening. Use the questions above to help you. Talk about the list in class. Write the finished guidelines on the board.

10 Using Your Language

Look at the verbs in these sentences:

1. She <u>knew</u> my cousin Brett.
2. We have <u>known</u> her for many years.

Both verbs show past time. Which verb is used with a helping word?

knew grew
and and
known **grown**

The verb <u>knew</u> is used by itself to show past time. The verb <u>known</u> is used with a helping word.

Look at the verbs in these sentences.

1. A cherry tree <u>grew</u> in our backyard.
2. Ed has <u>grown</u> such beautiful roses!

Both verbs show past time. Which verb is used with a helping word?

The word *grew* is used by itself to show past time. The word *grown* is used with a helping word.

Exercise A

Talk about the following in class. Use forms of *know* and *grow* in your sentences.

1. Something you know
2. Something you grew

Exercise B

Write each sentence. Use a form of the verb at the left for the box. Your sentences should show past time.

(know) **1.** We ☐ you would be late.

(grow) **2.** She has ☐ so tall!

(grow) **3.** The vine ☐ over the fence.

(know) **4.** Carol has ☐ some famous people.

(grow) **5.** This plant has ☐ too much.

Look at the verbs in these sentences.

1. I <u>saw</u> a shooting star last night.
2. Jack has <u>seen</u> all my baseball cards.

Both verbs show past time. Which verb is used with a helping word?

The verb *saw* is used by itself to show past time. The word *seen* is used with a helping word.

saw
or
seen?

Exercise C

Write each sentence. Use a form of the verb at the left for the box. Your sentence should show past time.

(see)   **1.** I have ☐ strange things.

(grow) **2.** Max ☐ up in Scranton.

(see)   **3.** Nobody ☐ us leave.

(see)   **4.** Luis has never ☐ a circus.

(know) **5.** I never ☐ my grandparents.

Have you ever written a report about dinosaurs? On the next few pages, you will read about a dinosaur. Decide for yourself whether "Believe It or Not" has any facts that could be part of a report. Perhaps the title has already helped you to decide.

BELIEVE IT OR NOT

"Ever see any dinosaur tracks?" asked the little old man.

"Yes," I answered. "I've seen dinosaur tracks in museums, but . . . "

"I don't mean in museums. I mean right where they happened. I mean not half a mile from here!"

I was sure the man was wrong, but I didn't want to be unkind. "You mean to say dinosaurs lived around here?" I asked.

He snorted impatiently. "Certainly! Seventy-five million years ago they did. Dinosaurs lived everywhere. They were the most successful creatures that ever lived on the face of the earth. They grew to be the biggest. They lived on this earth for a hundred million years. That is about ninety-five million more than people have been living here."

STRETCHING

I was in no mood to say anything in favor of human beings. Instead I asked a question, just to get away from him. "Where can I see these dinosaur tracks?" I glanced at my watch. "I don't have much time, but if they're not far from here . . ."

"Now you're talking sense," he said. "Just you mosey down the hill through that strand of trees till you get to the bottom. Then turn due south and keep going till you come to a pond. Won't take you ten minutes. On the edge of the pond you'll see the tracks I'm talking about."

"Well, thank you," I said, not believing a word of it, but figuring I didn't have anything to lose. "I'll go have a look." And I nodded good-bye.

I followed the old man's directions and soon found myself at the pond. I walked over to the edge of the pond. When I reached it, my hair stood on end. There were great big tracks, all right, leading into the water. The only trouble was, these tracks were in the mud, and they were fresh!

Naturally, as soon as the first shock was over, I told myself I couldn't very well be looking at fresh dinosaur tracks.

But then the surface of the pond began to heave and bubble like a pot of soup. Something began to rise up out of the water with the sound of a thousand people climbing out of bathtubs.

YOUR IMAGINATION

First a big head on a long neck, then a huge back, and finally part of a great thick tail.

I might not know much about dinosaurs, but I knew one when I saw one.

So I fainted.

Ever have a dinosaur spit water in your face? When I came to, that was what was happening to me. I looked up into the biggest pair of eyes I had ever seen. The huge creature had lowered his head in my direction at the end of about thirty feet of neck. He was making a chuckling sound. He had been spitting water in my face to bring me to. That's the way it seemed in this dream I was having. It just had to be a dream.

"Good grief!" I cried. "A dinosaur!"

"What did you expect, a catfish?"

"A talking dinosaur!" I said, and actually I felt better. "Well, at least now I *know* I'm only having a bad dream."

The dinosaur looked insulted. "Are you calling me a bad dream?"

"Well, I wouldn't call this a good one, when I'm dreaming I'm about to be eaten alive by a dinosaur!"

Now he looked amused. "Eaten alive? Don't be ridiculous. I'm not one of those meat-eating tyrannosauruses. I happen to be a brontosaurus, and I don't eat meat. I'm a vegetarian."

"This is ridiculous," I said. "You can't be real!"

"What do you mean? Listen, I've been real for seventy-five million years now. That's longer than any other living thing on this earth has been real!"

"Now look here," I said. I spoke pretty sharply, for me, but then I was annoyed. Even in a dream, when it came to making wild statements, a brontosaurus could only push me so far. "In the first place, you talk."

"What's wrong with that?"

"Animals can't talk, that's what's wrong with it. In the second place, there haven't been any living dinosaurs for millions of years. So don't stand there in that pond and tell me you're a living, talking dinosaur."

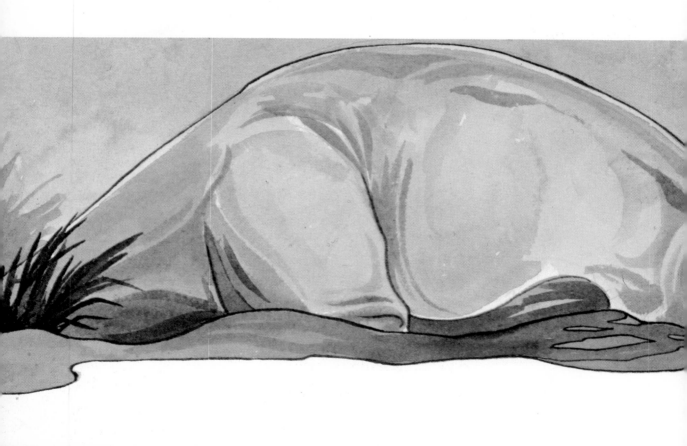

"Now, look at it this way," he said. "We dinosaurs lived over a period of a hundred million years. Doesn't it stand to reason we would develop a few outstanding minds in all that time. I don't like to blow my own horn, but it so happens that I'm the smartest dinosaur that ever came along. I have been able to figure out quite a few things that are still a little too much for your human minds."

"Such as?"

"Well, such as how to live for more than a hundred years without falling apart, the way humans do."

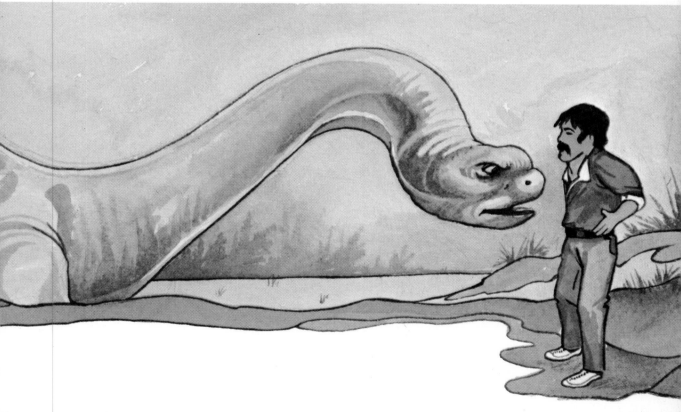

Obviously, he expected me to believe *anything.* I tried to keep a straight face.

"And how did you manage that?"

"I found out how to change my body in a way that would keep me from growing older."

"No kidding? That sounds almost incredible!"

"Yes, doesn't it," replied the dinosaur. "Of course, in doing so I had to become invisible — "

"In-*what*-able?"

"Invisible. But that has its advantages, too."

I took a deep breath. "Name one," I demanded.

"Well, I don't suppose I could have survived otherwise. Some of you crazy humans would have figured out a way to hunt me down and kill me by now, I expect."

"Now wait, just a minute," I said. "If you're invisible, how come I can see you?"

"I had the old man give you a shot with the old Inviso-Ray gun."

"You mean, he fixed it so I can see you?"

"That's right."

"And nobody else can?"

"Well, *he* can, but that's about all. You're lucky."

Was I? An invisible dinosaur who talks. Who would ever believe me?

SCOTT CORBETT

Fun with Facts 11

The writer of "Believe It or Not" had some fun with facts. Pretend that the meeting with the dinosaur really happened. Then get ready to s-t-r-e-t-c-h your imagination even more.

Exercise A

Pretend that you are a newspaper reporter. The person who met the dinosaur has just come to your office to tell you what happened. Write a report for tomorrow's paper. Remember to answer these questions: "Who?" "What?" "When?" "Where?" and "How?" Make your report look like a newspaper article.

Exercise B

Dinosaurs are interesting topics for reports. Many books have been written about them. Use the facts you find in a report to make up an imaginary story about you and a dinosaur.

The page numerals after each heading show you where to look if you need help with this review.

Identifying Facts and Opinions (230–231)

Write each sentence. After it, write whether it is a fact or an opinion.

1. NASA stands for National Aeronautics and Space Administration.
2. Astronauts lead dangerous lives.
3. Tourists can visit the John F. Kennedy Space Center.
4. The first international space mission was the Apollo Soyuz Test Project.
5. Space explorations may lead to the discovery of life in outer space.
6. There is nothing to be learned from space explorations.

Taking Notes for a Report (234–235)

Read the paragraphs below. Then take notes for part of a report on soil. Your notes should answer these questions: (1) What is soil and where is it found? (2) How is soil formed?

The loose surface of the earth is called soil. It is found almost everywhere, even on the bottoms of lakes and oceans. Soil is not found on top of high mountains where ice covers the ground.

Soil is formed when rocks break down to small pieces. Heat, cold, and rain help to soften rocks and make soil.

Getting Ideas in Order (236–237)

Arrange the ideas below under the proper main ideas that follow. Use a capital letter and a period to mark each fact about a main idea.

I. Abe Lincoln in his early years

II. Abe Lincoln as President

Born February 12, 1809, in Kentucky
First elected President in November 1860
Grew up in Indiana frontier
Helped end Civil War in 1865

Writing Titles (239)

Write these report titles correctly:

1. writing a verse for a card

2. the first american flag

3. helpful spiders

4. the flag of my state

Checking a Report (240–241)

The following report should be written in two paragraphs. It needs capital letters and punctuation marks. Write it correctly.

two meanings of a word

modern skyscrapers are tall city buildings most of the skyscrapers in the world are found in the united states there many people work in crowded cities the tall buildings do not use too much ground space most people do not know that the word *skyscraper* once meant something else a skyscraper was a sail used high on the mast of the old sailing ships both kinds of skyscrapers seem to scrape the sky

Identifying Facts and Opinions

Write each sentence. After it, write whether it is a fact or an opinion.

1. An octopus looks ugly.
2. An octopus has eight arms.
3. Every newspaper should have comic strips.
4. The sports page is the most interesting section of a newspaper.
5. A news story gives facts.
6. Charlie Brown is a character in a comic strip.
7. The camel is the best form of transportation in the desert.
8. Some camels have two humps.
9. Guinea pigs make good pets.
10. Guinea pigs are almost tailless.

Taking Notes for a Report

Read the paragraphs below. Then take notes for part of a report on helpful spiders. Your notes should answer these questions: (1) How do spiders help us? (2) Where do spiders live?

There are a few dangerous spiders, but most of them are harmless and help us. They eat flies, mosquitoes, and other insects. Some spider silk is used in telescopes.

Spiders live all over the world. They live in houses and barns and in fields. Some spiders live on mountaintops and others live under water. Wherever they live, most spiders are helpful.

Getting Ideas in Order

Arrange the ideas below under the proper main ideas that follow. Use a capital letter and a period to mark each fact about a main idea.

    I. Native American dolls made from animal skins

   II. Native American dolls made from corn husks, grass, or apples

Leather dolls stuffed with moss or dried grass
Apples dried and used for faces
Clothes for leather dolls made from soft deerskin
Corn husks tied and shaped like bodies

Writing Titles

Write these report titles correctly:

1. the praying mantis   **3.** my state motto

2. how to train a dog   **4.** the white house

Checking a Report

The following report should be written in two paragraphs. It needs capital letters and punctuation marks. Write it correctly.

ways of forecasting weather
birds are sometimes believed to be weather forecasters some people think birds always roost before a storm others think that if the birds fly south early, there will be an early winter some people say that a red sky in the evening is a sign that the next day will be fair a red sky in the morning is supposed to mean that rain is on the way do you believe in such weather signs

257

Skills Checkup

Writing Statements and Questions (17–18)

A. Write each group of words below as a statement:

1. our car is being repaired
2. these crayons are mine
3. the nest is empty
4. the roller rink is closed on Mondays
5. Rick has found a job

B. Write each group of words in Part A as a question.

Writing Titles (41)

Write these titles correctly:

1. a strange noise
2. riding the waves
3. a lucky guess
4. flying a kite

Finding Nouns in the Subject and the Predicate (58–59)

Write each sentence below. Draw a slash mark between the subject and the predicate. Then circle each noun you find in the subject and the predicate.

1. The small plane towed a glider.
2. The angry man shook his cane.
3. The spectators waved flags.
4. The sled just missed a tree.
5. The boy patched his jeans.

Addressing an Envelope (96)

Draw your own envelope and address it to a friend.

Using Alphabetical Order (118–119)

Write the numerals 1 to 12 on your paper. Then write the following words in alphabetical order.

potato	daisy	clock
teeth	water	beet
hamburger	lock	reward
lemon	flavor	glory

Writing Contractions (158–159)

Write each sentence. Change the underlined words in each sentence into a contraction.

1. The new supermarket <u>has</u> <u>not</u> opened yet.
2. <u>I am</u> waiting for my friend.
3. <u>We are</u> trying out a new recipe.
4. There <u>are</u> <u>not</u> enough books for everyone.
5. <u>We have</u> packed a picnic lunch.

Recognizing What the Characters Say (178–179)

Write the following conversation in the form of a play:

Dawn shouted, "Andy, come see what I've found!"
Andy called, "Where are you?"
Dawn said, "I'm in the attic."

Writing Directions in Order (210–211)

Look at the map on page 211. Then write directions for walking to the school from Washington Avenue and Fourth Street. Be sure to keep your ideas in order.

Writing Interesting Sentences

GRAMMAR	The Subject and the Predicate
	Questions and Statements
	Sentences with a Subject and a Verb
	Sentences with a Verb Followed by a Noun or a Pronoun
COMPOSITION	Making Sentences Grow
	Beginning Sentences in Different Ways
VOCABULARY	Words with Opposite Meanings
	Words with the Same Meaning
USAGE	Review

In this unit, you will review some important facts about the sentence. Then by making two different kinds of sentences grow, you will discover ways to make your sentences more interesting.

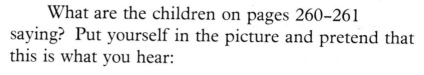

1 Speaking and Writing Sentences

What are the children on pages 260–261 saying? Put yourself in the picture and pretend that this is what you hear:

"Hello, Joe. Where have you been? We've been waiting for you."

"Hi, Kiyo. I've been to the library. Did I miss anything?"

Pretend that you are hearing the conversation, not reading it. How many spoken sentences did you hear? In speaking, how do you know when a sentence begins and ends? Exercise A will help you find out.

Exercise A

Divide into pairs and take turns holding a short conversation while the rest of the class listens. How can you tell when each sentence begins and ends? What did you notice besides the words?

When you hear people speak, you can easily recognize sentences. A pause follows each group of words spoken as a sentence. The up and down of the speaker's voice also helps you know where one sentence ends and another begins.

Written sentences are different. A punctuation mark is used in writing to show where a sentence ends. A capital letter shows where a new sentence begins.

Capital letters and punctuation marks help you understand sentences. What else is needed before a sentence can make sense? Read this group of words:

children the on met steps the

Do the words make sense? Words must be in a certain order to make a sentence. Now read the same group of words in sentence order:

The children met on the steps.

Exercise B

Write the following words in good sentence order. Begin each sentence with a capital letter. End it with a period or a question mark.

1. girls the a climbed tree
2. children watched race potato the
3. schools have most playgrounds
4. our has playground a pool
5. men the pitched horseshoes
6. grown-ups tennis played
7. boys did dance a folk
8. school our played soccer
9. paths along flowers grow the
10. families lunch ate a picnic
11. fathers babies pushed on swings
12. people the had fun

The Subject and the Predicate

Look at the first of the sentences you wrote for Exercise B on page 263. Does it look like this?

The girls climbed a tree.

Now look at the sentence again. What does the slash mark show?

The girls / climbed a tree.

The slash mark shows that a sentence has two parts: a subject and a predicate.

What is the part of the sentence to the left of the slash mark called? What does the subject of a sentence tell? The subject tells what the sentence is about.

What is the part of the sentence to the right of the slash mark called? What does the predicate tell? The predicate tells something about the subject.

You have just reviewed some important facts you learned about sentences in Unit One. Remember these facts as you practice writing better sentences in this unit.

CAREER CLUES

People enjoy coming to my shop. Many of my treats are made with eggs and flour. I am a _____.

1. Every sentence has two parts: a subject and a predicate.
2. The subject comes first in the sentence.
3. The subject tells what the sentence is about.
4. The predicate comes after the subject.
5. The predicate tells something about the subject.

264

Exercise A

Write the sentences below. Draw a slash mark between the subject and the predicate.

1. My brother answered the telephone.
2. The dog jumped over the fence.
3. The pigeons took a bath in a puddle.
4. The teacher piled the books on his desk.
5. A police officer blew her whistle.
6. The children played on the beach.
7. He ran to first base.
8. The clock ticked loudly.
9. We watched the boats.
10. Tina swam in the lake.

Exercise B

Look at the sentence parts below. Make sentences by adding the missing part—a subject or a predicate. Be sure to use capital letters and periods.

1. / read the paper.
2. The cat /
3. My friends /
4. / wanted a bike.
5. / helped me.
6. The doctor /
7. My teacher /
8. / joined a club.
9. / played with us.
10. My uncle /

Exercise C

Write three sentences of your own. Be sure that each sentence has a subject and a predicate.

3 Questions and Answers

In Unit One, you studied two different kinds of sentences. Show how much you remember by doing Exercise A.

Exercise A

Write the following sentences. Use capital letters correctly. If the sentence is a statement, use a period at the end. If the sentence is a question, use a question mark at the end.

1. our language has twenty-six letters
2. what do we call those letters
3. some people use pictures instead of words
4. what do you know about picture writing
5. can you read picture writing
6. other people use signs instead of words
7. they speak with their hands
8. can you speak with your hands
9. when did you learn the alphabet
10. the letters stand for sounds
11. we write with twenty-six letters
12. we speak with many sounds
13. a letter can stand for more than one sound
14. different letters can stand for the same sound
15. can you write a word for each sound

You can change the statements in Exercise A into questions.

Statement: Our language has twenty-six letters.
Question: Does our language have twenty-six letters?

Exercise B

Change these statements from Exercise A into questions. Remember to use capital letters and question marks.

1. They speak with their hands.
2. The letters stand for sounds.
3. A letter can stand for more than one sound.
4. Different letters can stand for the same sound.

You can answer each question in Exercise A by writing a statement.

Question: What do we call those letters?
Statement: We call those letters the alphabet.

Exercise C

Answer each question below with a statement. Remember to use capital letters and periods.

1. What do you know about picture writing?
2. Can you read picture writing?
3. Can you speak with your hands?
4. When did you learn the alphabet?
5. Can you write a word for each sound?

One Kind of Sentence

Read the sentences in the box. How are they alike?

SUBJECT	PREDICATE (VERB)
1. Buses	honk.
2. The taxis	move.
3. We	wait.

Each sentence has a subject and a predicate. In which sentence is the subject a noun? In which sentence does the noun follow a noun signal? In which sentence is the subject a pronoun?

 Exercise A

Look at the sentences in the box again. What other subjects could you use with *honk?* With *move?* With *wait?* Add a new subject as you read each sentence.

 Exercise B

Add a subject to each sentence below. Use the kind of subject called for at the left.

(noun alone)	**1.** ☐ melts.
(noun with article)	**2.** ☐ stopped.
(pronoun)	**3.** ☐ helped.

Now read the sentences in the box below. Pay special attention to the predicate.

SUBJECT	PREDICATE (VERB)
1. Buses	honked.
2. The taxis	were moving.
3. We	had waited.

In all three sentences, the predicate is made up of a verb that tells what a person or thing does.

In which two sentences does an auxiliary help the verb? Many of the sentences you speak and write have a predicate that is made up of a verb with or without an auxiliary.

Exercise C

Look again at the sentences above. What other verbs could you use with *Buses?* With *The taxis?* With *We?* Add a new verb as you read each sentence.

Exercise D

Add a verb to each of the subjects below. Use verbs with and without auxiliaries.

1. Chimneys ☐.
2. Fire ☐.
3. Dryers ☐.
4. Water ☐.
5. The snow ☐.
6. The flowers ☐.

5 Making Sentences Grow

Read the sentences in the box. They are the same kind of sentences you studied on pages 268–269.

SUBJECT	PREDICATE (VERB)
1. The children	played.
2. The man	walked.

You don't often speak and write such short sentences, do you? Here is one way to make these sentences grow.

1. The happy children played.
2. The old man walked.

What kind of word has been added to the subject in sentence 1? In sentence 2? What word does *happy* tell about, or describe. What word does *old* tell about, or describe? Words that describe a noun make a sentence more interesting. They do not change the pattern.

Exercise A

Write each sentence. Add a word that describes the noun in each sentence.

1. The ☐ women worked.
2. A ☐ child cried.
3. The ☐ car stalled.
4. The ☐ trees blew.

Look at the sentences in the box on page 270. Here is another way to make these sentences grow:

1. The children played quietly on the porch.
2. The man walked slowly down the street.

What words have been added to the predicate in sentence 1? In sentence 2? In sentence 1, what word do *quietly* and *on the porch* describe? In sentence 2, what word do *slowly* and *down the street* describe? Words that describe the verb make a sentence more interesting. They do not change the pattern.

Exercise B

Write each sentence. Add words that describe the verb.

1. The children ran.
2. The cars moved.
3. The dog barked.
4. The stars shone.
5. The rain fell.
6. The snow melted.
7. A man shouted.
8. The crowd laughed.
9. The train roared.
10. The bicycle stopped.

Exercise C

Write each sentence. Add words that describe both the subject and the predicate.

1. The cat slept.
2. Birds fly.
3. Flowers grow.
4. People walk.
5. The boys wave.
6. The people ran.
7. The driver shouted.
8. The book fell.
9. The players jumped.
10. The rabbit hopped.

6 Another Kind of Sentence

Look at the sentences in the box. How are they different from the sentences in the boxes on pages 268–269?

SUBJECT	PREDICATE (VERB + NOUN OR PRONOUN)
1. My sister	plays baseball.
2. Davey	hit the ball.
3. She	caught it.

A noun or a pronoun is often used in the predicate of a sentence. In sentence 1, what does my sister play? In sentence 2, what did Davey hit? In sentence 3, what did she catch? In sentences 1 and 2, the predicate is made up of a verb followed by a noun. In sentence 3, the verb is followed by the pronoun *it*. The noun or pronoun answers the question "Whom?" or "What?"

 Exercise A

Look at the sentences in the box. What other verbs could you use instead of *plays?* Instead of *hit?* Instead of *caught?* Use a different verb as you read each sentence. Then use a different noun or pronoun after the verb.

272

Take two sheets of paper. Then follow the directions below.

1. Draw this box on the first sheet:

SUBJECT	PREDICATE (VERB)

2. Draw this box on the second sheet:

SUBJECT	PREDICATE (VERB + NOUN OR PRONOUN)

3. Now write each sentence below in the box in which it belongs. Put the subject in the subject part and the predicate in the predicate part. Before you put a sentence into the second box, be sure that the noun after the verb answers "Whom?" or "What?"

a. Trees surrounded the cabin.

b. Skip chased the squirrel.

c. Dad is leaving tomorrow.

d. The clowns jumped into the car.

e. The holidays begin soon.

f. The skaters fell.

g. The contest has begun.

h. Tim won the race.

i. The dentist filled the hole.

j. A horse was grazing in the field.

k. The cat climbed the tree.

l. The girls found a cave.

7 Making Sentences Grow

Look at this sentence again:

SUBJECT	PREDICATE (VERB + NOUN)
My sister	plays baseball.

Now read this sentence:

My older sister plays baseball on Saturday with my brothers.

What words were added to the sentence "My sister plays baseball"? What word does *older* describe? What word do "on Saturday" and "with my brothers" describe? You can add words that describe to a sentence like the one shown in the box. The words make the sentence more interesting, but they do not change the pattern.

Exercise

Add words that describe to each sentence below. Add your words to the subject, to the predicate, or to both the subject and the predicate.

1. The car turned the corner.
2. The man cut the flowers.
3. The woman arranged the fruit.
4. The girls climbed the pole.
5. The children wanted food.

Now read these sentences. Pay special attention to the underlined words.

1. The <u>tired</u> players sat on the bench.
2. The <u>weary</u> players sat on the bench.

Has the meaning been changed in sentence 2? Do *tired* and *weary* have the same or almost the same meaning?

Two words sometimes have the same or almost the same meaning.

Words with the Same Meaning

Exercise C

Write another word that means the same or almost the same as these words:

friend	quick	small	correct
gift	unhappy	big	talk

Think about the different ways you learned to make sentences more interesting. Then edit the paragraph below. Remember to add words that describe. Begin the third sentence in a different way.

The children went for a walk. They saw a sailboat. They watched the animals at the zoo. The lions were eating. An elephant stared. Seals were diving. A seal flopped. The children had fun.

EDITING EXERCISE

10 Using Your Language

The chart below shows some of the verb forms you worked with in the last half of this book. Study the chart. Then do Exercises A and B. If you need help with a verb form, look it up in the index under "Using certain words."

SAY OR WRITE...	NOT...
1. He ran for home.	1. He run for home.
2. They came too late.	2. They come too late.
3. Sally has driven home.	3. Sally has drove home.
4. Bart has written a play.	4. Bart has wrote a play.
5. Maury did it.	5. Maury done it.
6. Maury has done it.	6. Maury has did it.
7. Tanya has gone home.	7. Tanya has went home.
8. Paco ate an apple.	8. Paco et an apple.
9. Paco has eaten an apple.	9. Paco has ate an apple.
10. We had taken a break.	10. We had took a break.
11. Edna saw me first.	11. Edna seen me first.
12. Edna had seen me first.	12. Edna had saw me first.
13. Greg knew the words.	13. Greg knowed the words.
14. Weeds grew everywhere.	14. Weeds growed everywhere.

 Exercise A

Read each sentence in the first column above. Then make up an example of your own.

278

Exercise B

Write each sentence. Use a form of the verb at the left for the box. Be sure to use a form that shows the past tense.

(go)   **1.** Bill has ☐ to summer camp.
(see)   **2.** I have ☐ you before.
(know)   **3.** Laurie said she ☐ his name.
(drive)   **4.** They have ☐ hard.
(take)   **5.** Stan ☐ a wrong turn.
(eat)   **6.** We have ☐ dinner.
(come)   **7.** The rain ☐ down hard.
(do)   **8.** Jane has ☐ well.
(grow)   **9.** The sky ☐ dark.
(write)   **10.** He had ☐ my name.

Review

The chart below reminds you when to use *is* or *are* and *was* or *were*.

he, she, it a singular noun	is, was
you, we, they a plural noun	are, were

Exercise C

Write each sentence. Use a word at the left for the box.

(are, is)   **1.** The cats ☐ in the corner.
(was, were) **2.** They ☐ happy to see us.
(are, is)   **3.** Your hands ☐ cold.
(was, were) **4.** It ☐ lots of fun.

279

Reviewing Your Skills

The page numerals after each heading show you where to look if you need help with this review.

Writing Sentences (262–263)

Write the following words in good sentence order. Begin each sentence with a capital letter. End it with a period or a question mark.

1. pianist the practiced hard
2. followed I directions the
3. open your shoelace is
4. friend your music can read

Making Sentences Grow (270–271)

A. Write each sentence. Add a word that describes the noun in each subject.

1. The ☐ canary sang.
2. The ☐ bear growled.
3. The ☐ roses bloomed.
4. A ☐ fountain splashed.
5. The ☐ bus stopped.

B. Write each sentence. Add a word that describes the verb.

1. The fly buzzed.
2. A cricket chirped.
3. The artist painted.
4. A fish jumped.
5. A rocket soared.

Making More Sentences Grow (274)

Add words that describe to each sentence below. Add your words to the subject, to the predicate, or to both the subject and the predicate. Make each sentence interesting.

1. Water flooded the basement.
2. Lightning struck a tree.
3. The girl saddled a horse.
4. The ranger spotted a fire.

Beginning Sentences in Different Ways (275)

Write each sentence. Put the underlined word or words at the beginning. If you put more than two words at the beginning, use a comma.

1. I go to camp every summer.
2. The librarian holds a story hour every Saturday morning.
3. Our class will give a play next week.
4. We went to the circus yesterday.

Using Your Language (164–165, 186–187, 214–215, 244–245, 278–279)

Write each sentence. Use a word at the left for the box.

(ran, run)   1. I ☐ for the school bus but missed it.

(came, come)   2. My cousins ☐ to visit me while I was in the hospital.

(are, is)   3. The artists ☐ selling their paintings.

(ate, eaten)   4. Haven't you ☐ yet?

(driven, drove)   5. My parents have ☐ to work.

(written, wrote) 6. Have you ☐ your report?

(did, done)   7. I ☐ my report yesterday.

(grew, growed)   8. My friends ☐ these plants.

Testing Your Skills

Writing Sentences

Write the following words in good sentence order. Begin each sentence with a capital letter. End it with a period or a question mark.

1. wrote poem this who
2. wasting time you are
3. Janice about trip her wrote
4. a nibbled the cheese mouse
5. brother my a taxi drives
6. girl whistled the softly

Making Sentences Grow

A. Write each sentence. Add a word that describes the noun in each subject.

1. The ☐ jet landed.
2. The ☐ wall collapsed.
3. The ☐ material tore.
4. A ☐ squirrel leaped.
5. The ☐ kitten purred.
6. The ☐ ladder shook.

B. Write each sentence. Add a word that describes the verb.

1. The bells rang.
2. A parrot squawked.
3. The engine sputtered.
4. The ice cream melted.
5. The trail ended.
6. The boy hummed.

Making More Sentences Grow

Add words that describe to each sentence below. Add your words to the subject, to the predicate, or to both the subject and the predicate. Make each sentence interesting.

1. A mechanic fixed the car.

2. A boy delivered the newspaper.

3. A police officer checked the door.

4. Children sang songs.

Beginning Sentences in Different Ways

Write each sentence. Put the underlined word or words at the beginning. If you put more than two words at the beginning, use a comma.

1. I pass your house on my way to school.

2. I clean my room on Saturdays.

3. We saw several deer on our hike.

4. I sold my last ticket yesterday.

5. The carpenters worked all afternoon.

Using Your Language

Write each sentence. Use a word at the left for the box.

(ate, eaten) **1.** You haven't ☐ anything.

(saw, seen) **2.** Have you ☐ the new building plans?

(grew, growed) **3.** The vine ☐ quickly.

(knew, knowed) **4.** I ☐ the answer.

(taken, took) **5.** The workers have ☐ a car pool.

(saw, seen) **6.** We ☐ that movie last week.

(gone, went) **7.** The locusts have ☐ away.

(did, done) **8.** Who ☐ this report?

Putting Words in Order (10–11)

Change the order of the words in each group below to make a sentence:

1. rained all it afternoon
2. blew bubble a the child
3. fireplace heats a cabin the
4. vacation doctor took a the
5. stacked grocer the cans the
6. thief the caught detectives

Using Capital Letters and Punctuation Marks (17–20)

Write each sentence. Use capital letters where they are needed. Use a period or a question mark at the end.

1. bamboo is a kind of grass
2. it grows very tall
3. where does it grow
4. i own a bamboo fishing pole
5. is the bamboo pole sturdy

Writing Titles (41)

Write these titles correctly:

1. one stormy night
2. a week in the mountains
3. my first job
4. a pony for everyone
5. traveling by train

Showing that Someone Is Speaking (42–43)

Write the sentences below. Use commas, capital letters, and quotation marks to show that someone is speaking.

1. ms. ramos asked who would like to go on a field trip

2. everyone shouted we would

3. ms. ramos asked where would you like to go

Finding Noun Signals (60)

Write each sentence below. Circle each article. Draw a line under the noun the article signals.

1. The butcher sliced the meat.

2. The girl strummed the guitar.

3. A bulldozer cleared the lot.

4. The principal thanked the speaker.

Writing Plural Nouns (62–63)

Write the plural form of each of the following singular nouns.

1. watch	**3.** branch	**5.** voice	**7.** pouch
2. star	**4.** beach	**6.** apple	**8.** wish

Writing Possessive Nouns (64–65)

Write each sentence below. Use the possessive form of the noun at the left for the box in each sentence.

(beaver)   **1.** A ☐ home is made of sticks and mud.

(sister)   **2.** My ☐ room is next to mine.

(Ranchers)   **3.** ☐ horses are well trained.

(dentist)   **4.** I waited in the ☐ office.

285

Skills Checkup

Recognizing Proper Nouns (67)

Write the pairs of nouns below. Use a capital letter to begin each proper noun.

1. cat — morris
2. monday — day
3. month — december
4. city — san francisco
5. alaska — state
6. friend — mary

Using Pronouns (70–72)

Write each sentence. Use pronouns in place of the underlined words.

1. Mark leaped high but <u>Mark</u> couldn't catch the ball.
2. The camel can live in the desert because <u>the camel</u> stores water in <u>the camel's</u> hump.
3. I found a scarf and took <u>the scarf</u> to the lost-and-found office.
4. The dog scratched <u>the dog's</u> ear.

Writing a Friendly Letter (88–96)

Put the five parts of the friendly letter in order. Write them correctly as parts of the same letter.

1. 22 winton street
   chicago illinois 60612
   november 15 19--
2. dear betsy
3. your friend
4. here is a picture i drew of myself don't i look sad i do miss you very much since you moved away i hope you will write to me soon
5. jane

Addressing Envelopes (96)

Draw your own envelope. Use your own address for the return address. Address the envelope to:

mr thomas cruz
315 north street
hawley pennsylvania 18428

Sending Postcards (101)

Cut out a 6-inch by 9-inch piece of paper. Draw or paste a picture on one side. Draw a line down the center of the other side. Write a note on the left side. Address it on the right side.

Using Alphabetical Order (118–119)

Write the numerals 1 to 12 on your paper. Then write the following words in alphabetical order.

chore	meeting	year
school	playground	bicycle
alphabet	hill	ghost
leaf	kite	ear

Using Guide Words (121)

Tell which of the following words you would find on a dictionary page with the guide words **pigeon** and **plantation.**

pitcher	plaster	parade
place	plan	pit
phone	pitchfork	plane
poison	pity	plant
plumber	piano	present

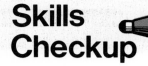
Using Your Language (24–25, 44–45, 76–77, 102–103, 130–131)

Write each sentence. Choose a word or words at the left for the box.

(a, an)   **1.** Who wants ☐ orange?

(any, no)   **2.** Your report hasn't ☐ title.

(I and Sid, Sid and I)   **3.** ☐ are building a fort.

(Them, Those)   **4.** ☐ riddles are hard.

Finding Verbs and Words That Help Verbs (154–157)

Write each sentence. Draw a line under the verb. Circle the helping word.

1. I am making a paper airplane.

2. The Robertsons are moving to Florida.

3. The actors are rehearsing their lines.

4. We are playing softball at noon.

5. This bread is getting stale.

Writing Contractions (158–159)

Write the following sentences. Draw a line under each contraction. Tell what two words make up the contraction.

1. I didn't receive any mail.

2. The squirrels aren't afraid of us.

3. The coach doesn't look happy.

4. Our team isn't doing well.

5. You're up at bat next.

Writing a Describing Paragraph (206–207, 212–213)

Choose one of the following. Write a describing paragraph about it. Choose your words carefully and arrange them in a certain order.

1. clouds   **3.** grass   **5.** a street

2. a merry-go-round   **4.** a barbecue   **6.** a cat

Correcting an Explaining Paragraph (208–209)

Write the sentences below as a paragraph in good explaining order.

1. Long ago people skated only on frozen lakes or ponds.

2. Ice-skating is a popular sport in the United States.

3. Many cities have skating clubs where children and grown-ups can learn to skate.

4. Skating is good exercise for everybody.

Getting Ideas in Order (236–237)

Arrange the ideas below under the proper main ideas that follow. Use a capital letter and a period to mark each fact about a main idea.

I. The days before the White House

II. The White House as the President's home

New York, the first home of a U.S. President
Philadelphia, the new capital
John Adams, the first President to live there
Some important changes since 1800

Handbook

This Handbook lists the important things you have learned in this book. It can help you remember what you have learned. It can also help you practice using what you have learned.

Topics are arranged in alphabetical order. The numerals following each topic show you where to look for more information.

Alphabetical Order *(118-121, 128)*

Words are put in alphabetical order by first letters. When words begin with the same letter, use the second letter to put the words in alphabetical order.

banana   **se**cret

monkey   **so**rry

zoo   **str**ong

Write these words in alphabetical order:

1. magic **2.** monkey **3.** meet **4.** milk

Apostrophe

1. An apostrophe is used to show ownership (64-65, 68):

   girl's skirt   girls' skirts   Ann's skirt

2. An apostrophe takes the place of the missing letter or letters in a contraction (158-159):

   I + am = I'm   are + not = aren't

Article *(60, 73, 74, 76-77, 268)*

The articles *a*, *an*, and *the* signal that a noun will follow. Sometimes a describing word will come between an article and a noun.

The little boy ate *an* apple.

Write each sentence. Circle each article.

1. A cloud is hiding the sun.
2. A puppy followed the children.

Capital Letters

Capital letters are used for:

1. The first word of a sentence (17-20, 93, 262-263, 266-267):

   A wolf howled.

2. The first word in the greeting of a letter (92):

   Dear Rosa,

3. The first word in the closing of a letter (94):

   Your friend,

4. The first word of a line of poetry:

   Up into the cherry tree
   Who should climb but little me?

5. The first word of a speaker in written converstion (42):

   Mom asked, "**W**ho will help me?"

6. The first, last, and all important words in titles (41, 239):

   A Squeak in the **N**ight

291

7. The word **I** (20)

8. Names of persons and pets (20, 67, 92):

   Cindy **J**ackson   **S**nowball

9. The words *Mother* and *Father* when used as names (68)

10. Titles of persons (92):

    Miss **M**rs. **M**r. **M**s. **D**r.

11. Initials:

    R. L. Thompson

12. Names of towns, cities, and states (67, 90):

    Wilton   **D**etroit   **M**aine

13. Names of countries:

    Mexico

14. Names of streets, avenues, and roads (90):

    Hudson **S**treet   **R**iver **R**oad

15. The words *Rural Route* and *Post Office Box* (90)

16. The abbreviations *Mrs., Mr., Ms., Dr., R. R.,* and *P. O.* (90)

17. The names of schools:

    Central **B**oulevard **S**chool

18. Names of days of the week, holidays, special days, and months (67, 90)

    Friday   Flag **D**ay
    Labor **D**ay   **J**anuary

19. Names of special groups:

    Pilgrims   **E**skimos

20. In an outline, to mark each fact about a main idea and for the first word of each main idea and each fact (236-237):

    I. **M**ain idea
       A. One fact
       B. Another fact

Write each sentence. Use capital letters where they are needed.

1. eileen will be eight years old on friday.
2. are you wearing a costume on halloween?
3. the pine avenue school is on pine avenue.
4. ms. sanders asked, "have you ever been to canada?"
5. my friend agnes is moving to denver in april.

Comma

A comma is used:

1. After the part that introduces the exact words of a speaker in written conversation (42):

   Mr. Johnson asked, "How are you today?"

2. Between the name of a town or a city and the name of a state (90):

   Boston, Massachusetts

3. Between the day of the month and the year in a date (90):

   January 1, 1900

4. After the greeting of a friendly letter (92):

   Dear Diane,

5. After the closing of a letter (94):

   Your cousin,

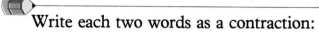

Write the following. Use commas where they are needed.

1. Albany New York
2. July 4 1776
3. Dear Aunt Kay
4. Your nephew

Contraction   *(158-159)*

A contraction is made up of two words written together with one or more letters left out. An apostrophe takes the place of the missing letter or letters.

1. Some contractions are made up of pronouns and helping words: *I* + *am* = *I'm*.
2. Some contractions are made up of a helping word and *not: have* + *not* = *haven't.*

Write each two words as a contraction:

1. are not   2. he is   3. you are   4. is not

Dictionary   *(See Unit Five.)*

Helping Word   *(154-157, 158-159, 164-165, 186-187, 214-215, 244-245, 269)*

1. The helping words *have, has,* and *had* are sometimes used with a form of the verb that ends in *-ed.* Some verbs have a special form that is used with the helping words *have, has,* and *had.*

Dora *has* finished her project.

She *has* made a terrarium.

2. The helping words *am, is, are, was,* and *were* are used with a form of the verb that ends in *-ing.*

Dora *is* working on a new project.

Write a sentence for each of these words. Use the helping word *have, has,* or *had* in each sentence.

1. started **2.** played **3.** made

Write a sentence for each of these words. Use the helping word *am, is, are, was,* or *were* in each sentence.

1. playing **2.** jumping **3.** keeping

Indenting   *(43, 93, 200, 204-205, 240)*

The first word of a paragraph is indented, or set in. Remember to indent the first word of every paragraph in a story, report, or body of a letter.

Letter Writing   *(See Unit Four.)*

Making Sentences Grow   *(16, 73, 160, 270-271, 274)*

You can make sentences grow by adding words to the subject and the predicate. These words make a sentence more interesting and more exact.

Waves crashed.
Towering waves crashed *noisily against the rocks.*

Make each sentence grow by adding describing words to the subject, to the predicate, or to both.

1. Insects crawled. **3.** Clowns tumbled.
2. Children play. **4.** Dogs barked.

Note Taking *(See Unit Nine.)*

Noun *(56-69, 73, 74, 76-77, 146, 268, 272-274)*

Words that name are called *nouns*. Nouns name persons, places, and things.

You can find nouns:

1. By position before a verb, as the subject:

   Geese / flew overhead.

2. By position after a verb, as part of the predicate:

   I / found a *dime*.

3. By position after the noun signals *a, an,* or *the:*

   The *dog* has a *bone*.

You can recognize nouns by their forms:

1. Nouns that name particular persons, places, or things are written with capital letters:

   Malibu Creek Park is in the *Santa Monica Mountains*.

2. Most nouns have a plural form, the form that shows more than one.

   a. Most nouns form the plural by adding *-s* to the singular:

      tree - trees   pen - pens

   b. Nouns ending in *s, x, z, ch,* and *sh* form the plural by adding *-es* to the singular:

      dish - dishes   fox - foxes

3. Most nouns have a possessive form.

   a. Singular nouns form the possessive by adding
     an apostrophe followed by an *s:*

     a cow's tail

   b. Most proper nouns form the possessive by
     adding an apostrophe and *s:*

     Leo's kite

   c. Plural nouns ending in *s* form the possessive
     by adding an apostrophe only:

     cows' tail

Write the plural form of each of these nouns:

1. branch   **3.** pencil   **5.** box
2. bush   **4.** beach   **6.** kiss

Write each group of words to show the possessive
form:

1. Martha☐ jacket
2. a mechanic☐ tools
3. mechanics☐ tools

Write each sentence. Underline each noun.

1. A scout raised the flag.
2. The artist cleaned her brushes.
3. The children blew bubbles.
4. Alex wrote a play.
5. The twins sang a duet.

Outline *(See Unit Nine.)*

Period

A period is used:

1. After a statement (17, 93, 262-263, 266-267):

   Honey is sweet.

2. After an abbreviation (90, 92):

   Mr. Mrs. Ms. Dr. R. R. P. O.

3. After an initial: Maria E. Sanchez.

4. In an outline, after each Roman numeral and capital letter used to mark an idea (236-237):

   I. Running shoes
      A. Lightweight
      B. Removable spikes

Predicate   *(12-13, 15, 16, 22-23, 148-149, 160, 264-265, 268-269, 271, 272-274)*

The predicate of a sentence tells something about the subject. The predicate usually follows the subject.

The pitcher / warmed up before the game.

Pronoun   *(70-72, 142, 158, 268, 272-273)*

A pronoun is a word that substitutes for a noun.

Write each sentence. Use pronouns in place of the underlined words.

1. Alex grabbed <u>Alex's</u> mitt as <u>Alex</u> leaped from the bench.

2. Donna left <u>Donna's</u> book in school.

Punctuation Marks   *(See Apostrophe, Comma, Period, Question Mark, and Quotation Marks.)*

Question *(18, 41, 266-267)*

A question is a sentence that asks something. It begins with a capital letter and ends with a question mark. Sometimes a question begins with a question word, such as *Who, What, When, Where, How,* and *Why.*

Where are you going**?**

Question Mark *(18, 41, 266-267)*

A question mark is used after a sentence that asks a question.

Are we having a test today**?**

Write each question correctly:

1. where is your book
2. is this book yours

Write four questions. Use one of these question words to begin each question:

Who   What   When   Where   How   Why

Quotation Marks *(42-43, 178)*

Quotation marks are used around the exact words of a speaker in written conversation.

Bob said, **"**Help me carry this package.**"**

Write each sentence below as the exact words of a speaker. Make up a name for each speaker.

1. Please be seated.
2. Is this the bus to Plainview?

Sentence Parts *(12-14, 16, 22-23, 148, 264-265, 268-274)*

Every sentence has a subject and a predicate. The subject (to the left of the slash mark) tells whom or what the sentence is about. The predicate (to the right of the slash mark) tells something about the subject.

This guitar / needs new strings.

Write each sentence. Draw a slash mark between each subject and predicate.

1. Roses grew along the fence.
2. The flag waved in the breeze.
3. A fly buzzed near my ear.

Statement *(17, 266)*

A statement is a sentence that tells something. A statement begins with a capital letter and ends with a period.

Tiny ants climbed the stalk.

Write these statements correctly:

1. the doctor removed the splinter
2. my best friend is moving away

Subject *(12-14, 16, 22, 74, 148, 165, 264-265, 268-270, 272-274)*

The subject of a sentence tells what or whom the sentence is about.

Tiny ants / climbed the stalk.

Using Words

A, An (76-77, 130)

Use *a* before a word that begins with a consonant sound. Use *an* before a word that begins with a vowel sound.

I saw *an* airplane and *a* helicopter.

Any, No (102, 130)

Do not use the words *no* and *not* in the same sentence when only one of them is needed.

WRONG: I didn't have no lunch.

RIGHT: I didn't have any lunch.

Ate, Eaten (214, 228)

The word *ate* is used by itself to show past time. The word *eaten* is used with a helping word.

I *ate* my sandwich.

Have you *eaten* your sandwich?

Came, Come (164, 278)

The word *came* is used by itself to show past time. The word *come* is used with a helping word to show past time.

The circus *came* to town.

Has the newspaper *come*?

Did, Done (186, 228)

The word *did* is used by itself to show past time. The word *done* is used with a helping word.

Marty *did* his homework.

I have *done* my homework, too.

Drove, Driven (186, 228)

The word *drove* is used by itself to show past time. The word *driven* is used with a helping word.

Mother *drove* us to school.

She has *driven* us often.

Grew, Grown (244, 278)

The word *grew* is used by itself to show past time. The word *grown* is used with a helping word.

The sunflowers *grew* tall.

They have *grown* tall quickly.

Is, Are (165, 279)

Use *is* with a singular subject. Use *are* with a plural subject.

This book *is* mine.

Those books *are* his.

Knew, Known (244, 278)

The word *knew* is used by itself to show past time. The word *known* is used with a helping word.

I *knew* the answer.

We have *known* each other a long time.

Naming Yourself Last (44-45, 130)

When talking about other persons and yourself, always name yourself last.

Sara and I painted the bookcase.

Those books belong to *Sara and me.*

Ran, Run *(164, 278)*

The word *ran* is used by itself to show past time. The word *run* is used with a helping word to show past time.

I *ran* in the first race.

I have never *run* in a meet before.

Saw, Seen *(245, 278)*

The word *saw* is used by itself to show past time. The word *seen* is used with a helping word.

I *saw* that movie.

My brother has *seen* it, too.

Them, Those *(103, 130)*

Those can be used to signal a noun. *Them* is never used to signal a noun.

WRONG: Them birds are robins.

RIGHT: Those birds are robins.

Took, Taken *(215, 278)*

The word *took* is used by itself to show past time. The word *taken* is used with a helping word.

Someone *took* my book.

I have *taken* a free sample.

Was, Were *(165, 279)*

Use *was* with a singular subject. Use *were* with a plural subject.

The kitten *was* hungry.

The kittens *were* hungry.

Went, Gone (214, 278)

The word *went* is used by itself to show past time. The word *gone* is used with a helping word.

The rash *went* away.

Dad has *gone* to the store.

Wrote, Written (186, 278)

The word *wrote* is used by itself to show past time. The word *written* is used with a helping word.

I *wrote* a poem.

Have you *written* your friend?

Write each sentence. Use a word at the left for the box.

(a, an)   1. Will you peel ☐ orange for me?
(any, no)   2. There isn't ☐ mustard left.
(ate, eaten)   3. Who has ☐ my sandwich?
(came, come)   4. Grandpa has ☐ for a visit.
(did, done)   5. The carpenter has ☐ a good job.
(driven, drove) 6. They have ☐ to the game.
(grew, grown)   7. The corn has ☐ tall.
(are, is)   8. Sweets ☐ bad for your teeth.
(knew, known)   9. Have you ☐ her a long time?
(I and Dad,   10. ☐ are planning a surprise.
  Dad and I)
(ran, run)   11. My cat has ☐ away.
(saw, seen)   12. No one had ☐ the burglar.
(them, those)   13. Who baked ☐ pies?
(taken, took)   14. We have ☐ the wrong road.
(was, were)   15. The answers ☐ wrong.
(gone, went)   16. Where has everybody ☐ ?
(written, wrote) 17. I have ☐ to my pen pal.

Verb *(146-165, 186-187, 214-215, 244, 245, 268-269, 271-274)*

A verb usually tells what a person or thing does or is. You can often find verbs by their position in the sentence:

1. After the subject:

   The horse / *leaped* the fence.

2. After a helping word:

   The rancher has *called* for help.

   A cowhand is *chasing* the horse.

You can recognize verbs by their forms:

1. Most verbs that show past time end in *-ed: play —played.*

2. The form of the verb that ends in *-ing* is used with the helping words *am, is, are, was,* and *were: am helping.*

Write each sentence. Underline the verb. Circle the helping word if there is one.

1. The noodles have cooked long enough.
2. The band is playing a march.
3. The librarian told a story.
4. The puppy is chewing your slipper.

Vocabulary

Compound Words (75)

Sometimes two words are put together to make one compound word.

note + book = notebook

Write three different compound words from these words:

school   foot   book   lace   ball   shoe

Sound Words (*162-163*)

Certain words may make you think of certain sounds.

Roosters crow.   Rusty hinges squeak.

What kind of sound do the words at the left make you think of? Read each sentence at the right. Then decide which word belongs in which box.

(purred)   **1.** The barber ☐ off my bangs.
(spattered) **2.** A jet ☐ by overhead.
(streaked)   **3.** The cat ☐ as it lay on my lap.
(snipped)   **4.** Mud ☐ the windshield.

Word Opposites (*276*)

Two words sometimes have opposite meanings.

hot - cold   inside - outside

Write the word opposites in the list below:

tiny   large   rough
smooth   new   old

Words with the Same Meaning (*277*)

Two words sometimes have the same or almost the same meaning.

noisy - loud   peaceful - calm

Write another word that means the same or almost the same as these words:

1. happy   **2.** large   **3.** sad

More Practice

Putting Letters in Order (8-9)

Change the order of the letters in each group below to make the name of a drink:

1. ewtar   **3.** lmik   **5.** ate

2. eciju   **4.** doas   **6.** caoco

Putting Words in Order (10-11)

Change the order of the words in each group below to make a sentence:

1. climbed the hikers the hill
2. a found the girl quarter
3. Anna me phone on the called
4. birds I book about read a
5. fence sat rooster a on the

Dividing Sentences Into Two Parts (12-13)

Write the sentences below. Draw a slash mark between the subject and the predicate.

1. The little kitten crawled up the curtain.
2. The pebble skipped across the water.
3. A blue jay carried a worm to its nest.
4. A girl pulled the wagon.
5. My aunt plays the piano well.
6. A car parked near the tree.
7. My sister finished the race in third place.
8. The sun shone brightly.

More Practice

Finding Key Words (*14-15*)

Write each sentence. Underline the key word in the subject once. Underline the key word in the predicate twice.

1. The dog ran down the stairs.
2. My bird flew out of its cage.
3. The tiger growled at the man.
4. The girls paddled the canoe.
5. The bell rang at noon.

Writing Statements and Questions (*17-18*)

A. Write each group of words below as a statement:

1. grandma will come for my birthday
2. my brother is studying his lessons
3. your mother is working today
4. it is snowing hard
5. you were playing checkers

B. Write each group of words in Part A as a question:

Using Capital Letters (*20*)

Write each sentence. Use capital letters where they are needed. Use a period or question mark at the end.

1. i have a friend named gerry
2. gerry's dog ruff is very smart
3. ruff can do many tricks
4. gerry and i like to play with ruff
5. may i feed ruff

308

Writing Titles (*41*)

Write each title. Use capital letters where they are needed.

1. our new car
2. fun in the sun
3. a trip to the beach
4. building a birdhouse
5. lions and tigers
6. a surprise for my birthday

Showing That Someone Is Speaking (*42-43*)

Write the sentences below. Use commas, capital letters, and quotation marks to show that someone is speaking.

1. craig said i see the seals
2. dolly said there's a tiger in that cage
3. craig asked can we pet the ponies
4. dolly said i love going to the zoo

Using Your Language (*44-45*)

Write each sentence. In sentences 1 to 3, use someone's name and the word *I* for the box. In sentences 4 to 6, use someone's name and the word *me*.

1. ☐ baked a cake.
2. ☐ studied our lessons together.
3. ☐ cleaned up the mess.
4. The police officer thanked ☐ .
5. Mr. Avery gave the package to ☐ .
6. A nurse helped ☐ .

More Practice

Finding Nouns in the Subject and in the Predicate (58-59)

Write each sentence below. Put a slash mark between the subject and the predicate. Draw a line under each key word in the subject. Circle each noun in the predicate.

1. The pupil wrote a poem.
2. A monkey ate the banana.
3. My father has a new job.
4. A little girl owns that bike.
5. The teacher explained the lesson.

Finding Noun Signals (60)

Write each sentence below. Circle each article. Draw a line under the noun the article signals.

1. A squirrel buried the nuts.
2. A tree fell to the ground.
3. The cow grazed in the pasture.
4. The game lasted an hour.
5. A magazine is on the table.

Writing Plural Nouns (62-63)

Write the plural form of each of the following singular nouns:

1. pencil   6. duck
2. fox   7. wish
3. pouch   8. bar
4. bear   9. punch
5. bush   10. house

Writing Possessive Nouns (*64-65*)

Write each sentence below. Use the possessive form of the noun at the left for the box in each sentence.

(neighbor)   **1.** The cat sat on our ☐ fence.
(uncle)   **2.** My ☐ car is at the gas station.
(friend)   **3.** Your ☐ birthday is tomorrow.
(pet)   **4.** Our ☐ name is Snuffy.
(sister)   **5.** Your ☐ friend is at the door.
(scientists)   **6.** The ☐ experiments were successful.

Recognizing Proper Nouns (*67*)

Write the pairs of nouns below. Use a capital letter to begin each proper noun.

1. whale - moby dick
2. chicago - city
3. month - october
4. sandy - horse
5. day - tuesday
6. wyoming - state
7. holiday - thanksgiving
8. rico - friend
9. yorktown - town
10. cousin - maria

Using Pronouns (*70-72*)

Write each sentence. Use pronouns in place of the underlined words.

1. Mr. Andrew had left <u>Mr. Andrew's</u> hat in the office.
2. The necklace has real diamonds in <u>the necklace</u>.
3. <u>The diamonds</u> are worth hundreds of dollars.
4. <u>Robins</u> like to eat birdseed.
5. I built a birdhouse for <u>the robins</u>.

More Practice

Writing Headings Correctly (*90-91*)

Write these headings correctly:

1. lawrence school
   cleveland ohio 44118
   january 19 19___
2. 94 tulane drive
   knoxville tennessee 37914
   november 23 19___
3. 977 chester drive
   colter bay wyoming 83001
   august 3 19___
4. r r 2
   springfield virginia 22150
   march 15 19___

Writing Greetings Correctly (*92*)

Write these greetings correctly:

1. dear terry
2. dear mr melon
3. dear aunt rita
4. dear sid
5. dear father
6. dear david
7. dear mrs angus
8. dear dr cluny

Writing Closings Correctly (*94-95*)

Write these closings correctly:

1. yours truly
2. love always
3. your best friend
4. your niece
5. your pen pal
6. your grandson
7. your buddy
8. your daughter

Writing a Friendly Letter (*88-95*)

Put the five parts of the friendly letter in order. Write them correctly as parts of the same letter.

1. your friend
2. 896 darling avenue
   portland maine 04103
   july 29 19___
3. gus
4. my mom bought a house in the mountains we are going to visit it next week i would like you to come with us we can go swimming and fishing whenever we want to let me know if you can come
5. dear frank

Addressing Envelopes (*96*)

A. Miss Hadley is sending a letter to Mr. Griffin. Draw an envelope. Fill in the return address and the address.

miss greta m hadley   mr n d griffin
444 wadley road   60 stewart drive
macon georgia 31210   jackson mississippi 39208

B. Draw an envelope and address it to a friend.

More Practice

Using Your Language (*24-25, 44-45, 76-77, 102-103, 130-131*)

Write each sentence. Use a word at the left for the box.

(Dad and I, I and Dad)   **1.** ☐ polished the car.
(a, an)   **2.** He left ☐ hour ago.
(any, no)   **3.** I didn't eat ☐ candy.
(I and Lee, Lee and I)   **4.** ☐ walked to the beach.
(a, an)   **5.** We took ☐ early train.
(Them, Those)   **6.** ☐ starfish can grow new arms.

Recognizing Verbs (*148-149*)

Write each sentence. Put a slash mark between the subject and the predicate. Draw a line under the verb.

1. Paula paddled the canoe.
2. Eddie threw a Frisbee.
3. Janice lives next door to me.
4. My grandmother bought a new car.
5. Her dog barks at strangers.

Finding Verbs and Words That Help Verbs (*154-157*)

Write each sentence. Draw a line under the verb. Circle the helping word.

1. Florence is riding her bicycle.
2. Your father is waiting outside for you.
3. The rabbit has eaten the lettuce.
4. The alarm clock is ticking loudly.
5. Your friends are ringing the doorbell.

Writing Contractions (*158-159*)

Write the following sentences. Draw a line under each contraction. Tell what two words make up the contraction.

1. She's doing her homework.
2. They're playing baseball at the field.
3. I've finished my chores.
4. We're buying a new car.
5. I'm going to a new school next year.
6. You've called the wrong person.

Writing Titles (*239*)

Write these report titles correctly:

1. early american art
2. how to build a tree house
3. pets in the home
4. fun and games with words
5. space travel

Writing Sentences (*262-263*)

Write the following words in good sentence order. Begin each sentence with a capital letter. End it with a period or a question mark.

1. tired soccer was the player
2. story I short a wrote
3. growled me the at tiger
4. our painted neighbor house his
5. carried we the boxes

More Practice

Beginning Sentences in Different Ways (*275*)

Write each sentence. Put the underlined words at the beginning. If you put more than two words at the beginning, use a comma.

1. Dad makes breakfast <u>every morning</u>.
2. I will be in the fourth grade <u>next year</u>.
3. Mom jogs three miles <u>before work</u>.
4. My sister plays soccer <u>every Tuesday afternoon</u>.
5. Summer vacation begins <u>next week</u>.

Using Your Language (*164-165, 186-187, 214-215, 244-245, 278-279*)

Write each sentence. Use a word at the left for the box.

(written, wrote)   **1.** Have you ☐ to Bella since she moved?

(ran, run)   **2.** We ☐ in the mile relay race.

(driven, drove)   **3.** Mom has ☐ in the new car.

(are, is)   **4.** The authors ☐ signing books.

(ate, eaten)   **5.** Have we ☐ this before?

(did, done)   **6.** I ☐ my chores early this morning.

(grew, growed)   **7.** Sue's hair ☐ very long this summer.

(was, were)   **8.** All the third graders ☐ in the play.

(came, come)   **9.** The newspaper ☐ late yesterday.

(gone, went)   **10.** My friends have ☐ home.

(taken, took)   **11.** You have ☐ my seat.

(knew, knowed)   **12.** I ☐ which trail to take.

Index

Index

Index

Index

Index

Index

Index

Index

Index

CREDITS

Design: Thomas Vroman Associates, Inc.

Developmental Writer: George Balish

Editorial: Eleanor Jacovina, Editorial Director; Eleanor Franklin, Project Editor

Katherine Rowen, Assistant Editor; Theresa Ladimir, Department Assistant

Design: Leslie Bauman, Design Director; Ruth Riley, Design Supervisor.

Production: Trudy Pisciotti, Production Manager; Barbara Arkin, Production Director.

Art Coordinator: Jennifer Vroman; Illustrators: Melanie Arwin, pp. 47, 52; Carolyn Bracken, pp. 6, 7, 8, 217, 218, 220, 221, 230, 253; Frank Crump, p. 135; Marion Ebert, p. 89; Allen Eitzen, pp. 105, 107; Diane Paterson, pp. 132, 133, 134; Karen Pellaton, pp. 101, 117; Albert J. Pucci, pp. 4, 32, 33, 56, 57, 166; Chris Santoro, pp. 247, 248, 249, 250, 251, 252; Jerry Smath, pp. 175, 189, 190; Pat Stewart, pp. 9, 17, 23, 24, 25, 61, 75; Tom Vroman, p. 147.

Photo Credits: Photo Research—Elyse Rieder; Cover—James Amos, Photo Researchers; pp. 2-4, Allan Philiba; pp. 30-32, The Photo Works; pp. 54-56, Courtesy of Greyhound Bus Company; pp. 84-86, The American Museum of Natural History; pp. 114-116, Courtesy of Washington Area Convention and Visitors Bureau; pp. 144-146, Joachim Messerschmidt, F.P.G.; pp. 172-174, Martin Jackson; pp. 198-200, Guy Gillette, Photo Researchers; p. 207, Dick Dietrich, F.P.G.; pp. 228-230, Dennis Hallinan, Alpha; pp. 260-262, John Lei.

ACKNOWLEDGMENTS

Every reasonable effort has been made to trace the owners of copyright materials in this book, but in some instances this has proven impossible. The publishers will be glad to receive information leading to more complete acknowledgments in subsequent printings of this book, and in the meantime extend their apologies for any omissions.

"The Loudest Noise in the World," pages 104 ff. From THE LOUDEST NOISE IN THE WORLD by Benjamin Elkin and James Daugherty. Copyright © 1954 by Benjamin Elkin and James Daugherty. Reprinted by permission of Viking Penguin Inc.
Dictionary entry, page 116. From SCOTT, FORESMAN BEGINNING DICTIONARY by E. L. Thorndike and Clarence L. Barnhart. Copyright © 1976 by Scott, Foresman and Company. Reprinted by permission.
Dictionary entries, pages 122, 124, 125. By permission. From Webster's Beginning Dictionary © 1980 by G & C. Merriam Co., Publishers of the Merriam-Webster Dictionaries.
Dictionary entries, pages 123, 126. From BEGINNING DICTIONARY, Macmillan Publishing Co., Inc. Copyright © 1976, 1975 Macmillan Publishing Co., Inc. Reprinted by permission of the publisher.

"The Parrot," page 132 and "The Question Mark," page 134. From The Zoo That Grew by Ilo Orleans and Harold Berson. Copyright © 1960 by the authors. Reprinted by permission of Friede Orleans Jaffe, Harry Z. Walck, Inc., a division of the David McKay Company, Inc.

"Eletelephony," page 133. From TIRRA LIRRA: Rhymes Old and New by Laura E. Richards, by permission of Little Brown and Co. Copyright 1930, 1932 by Laura E. Richards. Copyright renewed © 1960 by Hamilton Richards.

"I Speak, I Say, I Talk," page 163. From Volume I, Childcraft, The How and Why Library. © 1979 World Book-Childcraft International, Inc.

"Feeding the Fish," pages 188 ff. From Things That Sometimes Happen. Copyright, 1970, by Avi Wortis.

"Stringbeans," pages 216 ff. Abridgement and adaptation of "Stringbeans" in BUSYBODY NORA by Johanna Hurwitz. Text Copyright © 1976 by Johanna Hurwitz. By permission of William Morrow & Company.

"Believe It or Not," pages 246 ff. Adapted from EVER RIDE A DINOSAUR? by Scott Corbett. © 1969 by Scott Corbett. Reprinted by permission of Holt, Rinehart and Winston, Inc.